-6mm -5mm -4mm -3mm -2mm -1mm

1 mm 2 mm 3 mm 4 mm 5 mm 6

-6mm -5mm -4mm -3mm -2mm -1mm

-6mm -5mm -4mm -3mm -2mm -1mm

Alignment – check the front-to-back alignment by holding an Alignment Job up to the light to view the crosshairs.

Tolerance: 1 mm in any of 4 directions

Frequency: every Alignment Job, checking all positions across the web

1 mm 2 mm 3 mm 4 mm 5 mm 6 mm

e flush
th edge

4.25 mm white
above line

Book Block Fan – fan book block to check for shading, toner smears or flaking, wrinkling, oil spots, mill splices, spots or lines on text or halftones or any other print defects

Frequency: one book block per delivery, alternating stacks (one book per stacker load on the Xeroxes)

line flus
with edg

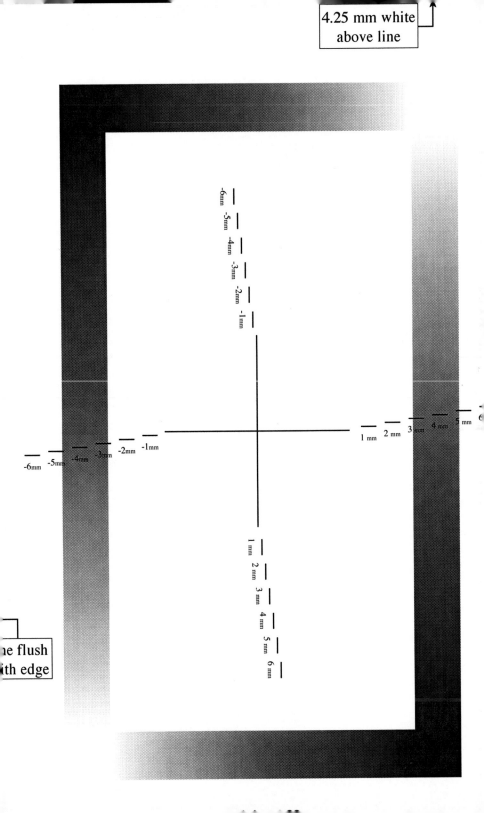

4.25 mm white
above line

he flush
ith edge

4.25 mm white
above line

line flus
with edg

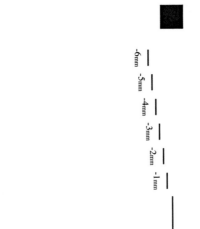

4.25 mm white
above line

-6mm -5mm -4mm -3mm -2mm -1mm

1 mm 2 mm 3 mm 4 mm 5 mm 6

Alignment – check the front-to-back alignment by holding an Alignment Job up to the light to view the crosshairs.
    Tolerance: 1 mm in any of 4 directions
    Frequency: every Alignment Job, checking all positions across the web

ne flush
ith edge

Book Block Fan – fan book block to check for shading, toner smears or flaking, wrinkling, oil spots, mill splices, spots or lines on text or halftones or any other print defects

Frequency: one book block per delivery, alternating stacks (one book per stacker load on the Xeroxes)

CREDO

*The Apostles' Creed Explained
for Today*

Hans Küng

SCM PRESS LTD

First British edition published 1993
by Lightning Source Inc.

Fifth Impression 2005

Phototypeset by Intype, London
Printed and bound in Great Britain by
Mackays of Chatham PLC, Chatham, Kent

Contents

Credo – Today?   ix

Symbolum Apostolorum – The Apostles' Creed   xiv

I. God the Father: The Image of God and the
   Creation of the World   7

   1. Can we believe it all?   7
   2. What does 'believe' mean?   10
   3. Does the modern criticism of religion still hold?   12
   4. Belief in creation and cosmology – a contradiction?   15
   5. Can we believe in the creator God in the age of
      cosmology?   18
   6. The transition to life – an intervention by the creator
      God?   21
   7. Can we believe in the creator in the age of biology? 24
   8. Can we believe in God the 'Father', the 'almighty'?   26
   9. The common belief in God of the three prophetic
      religions   29

II. Jesus Christ: Virgin Birth and Divine Sonship   33

   1. Do we believe in a virgin birth?   34
   2. Belief in Christ in the age of psychotherapy   35
   3. Virgin birth – a biological fact?   41
   4. The political dimension of Christmas   45
   5. Belief in Christ or Krishna – is it the same thing?   47
   6. The challenge of the Buddha   49
   7. What Jesus and Gautama have in common   51
   8. Where Jesus and Gautama differ   53
   9. The Illuminated and the Crucified   55
  10. What does it mean to say that God has a Son?   56
  11. The meaning of incarnation   59

III. The Significance of Christ's Cross and Death 62

  1. In the cross of co-ordinates of the world religions 62
  2. The image of the sufferer *par excellence* 64
  3. A political revolutionary? 69
  4. An ascetic and monk? 71
  5. A pious Pharisee? 73
  6. Not the usual scholastic disputes, but confrontation
    and conflict 77
  7. In whose name? 78
  8. Who is to blame for Jesus' death? 80
  9. A crucified God? 85
  10. A test case for the question of theodicy: God in
     Auschwitz? 89
  11. Meaningless suffering cannot be understood
     theoretically, but must be endured in trust 91

IV. Descent into Hell – Resurrection – Ascension 95

  1. The image of the Risen One 95
  2. Descent into the underworld? 97
  3. An ascension? 100
  4. Do we believe in the empty tomb? 103
  5. Is resurrection from the dead un-Jewish? 105
  6. Do we believe in the resurrection of the One? 107
  7. What 'resurrection' does and does not mean 110
  8. Just one life or several? 113
  9. Radicalization of belief in the God of Israel 117
  10. A decision of faith 119

V. Holy Spirit: Church, Communion of Saints and
   Forgiveness of Sins 122

  1. Spiritualized painting 122
  2. What does Holy Spirit mean? 124
  3. Pentecost – a historical event? 126
  4. Should we remain in the church? 129
  5. What is the church? 132
  6. The church – apostolic but undemocratic? 134
  7. What does catholic mean today? What does
    evangelical mean? 136

8. A 'holy' church?   139
9. What does 'communion of saints' mean?   141
10. What does 'forgiveness of sins' mean?   144
11. Why is there no mention of the Trinity in the Apostles' Creed?   150
12. How do we talk of Father, Son and Spirit?   152
13. Spirit of freedom   155

VI. Resurrection of the Dead and Eternal Life   157

1. Heaven as an artistic illusion   158
2. The heaven of faith   161
3. The physical end of the world – brought about by human beings   163
4. World history as the world's judgment?   167
5. Do we believe in the devil?   170
6. An eternal hell?   171
7. Purgatory and unexpiated guilt   176
8. Human destiny   178
9. Will we see only God?   180
10. Another attitude to dying   184
11. What are we on earth for?   188

Notes   191
Books by Hans Küng   195

Credo – Today?

How many people are still interested in the traditional Christian faith? Many call themselves religious, but not Christian; many call themselves Christians, but not church members. But vigorous controversies about individual traditional statements of faith, above all in the Catholic Church, are attracting attention even outside the church walls and show how far the age-old basic questions of the Christian creed are from being settled. There is a public dispute about the understanding of key statements even in the traditional creed, the 'Apostles' Creed': 'Born of the Virgin Mary. Risen from the dead. Descended into hell. Ascended into heaven.' And once again the bitter fight is being fought between the *magisterium* and contemporary theology about correct interpretation. Here false alternatives are often posed, between 'objective' church teaching and subjective-psychological metaphorical interpretation.

One thing is clear: today, happily, no one can be forced to believe any longer. However, many contemporaries would very much like to believe, though they cannot believe as people did in antiquity and the Middle Ages, or at the time of the Reformation. Too much has changed in the overall constellation of our time. Too much in Christian faith seems alien, seems to contradict the natural sciences and the humanities and indeed the humane impulses of our time. This book is meant to help here. What Pope John XXIII in 1962 called the 'springboard' for Vatican II in the famous address with which he opened the Council can also be called the springboard for this book. It is not concerned with 'the discussion of this or that basic article of church doctrine in a verbose repetition of the teaching of the fathers and of theologians old and new. It may be taken for granted that we are always aware of these teachings and shaped by them.' But it is concerned with 'a leap forward, towards a thorough understanding of doctrine and a training of consciences, to some degree towards more perfect accord with and fidelity to the true doctrine, albeit studied and presented in the form of research and expressed in line with a modern way of thinking'.

The explanation of the Apostles' Creed which I have presented here is indebted to this spirit of the Council. It is meant
– not to be a personal and arbitrary interpretation, but an interpretation on the basis of scripture of the articles of faith formulated in this 'creed';
– not to be an esoteric or sterile dogmatic interpretation, but one which takes seriously the questions of contemporaries; it is no arcane knowledge only for those who already believe, but understandable, as far as possible, also for those who do not believe, without academic gestures and stilted language; with no assertions which are manifestly contrary to reason but an argument for trust in a reality beyond the limits of pure reason;
– not to favour any special church tradition, nor, conversely, to surrender to a particular psychological school of thought, but to take its bearings in unconditional intellectual honesty by the gospel, i.e. by the original Christian message as it can be described today by means of historical-critical research;
– not to encourage any confessional ghetto mentality, but to strive for ecumenical breadth with which the three great Christian churches can feel in sympathy and which will also make possible a bridge to dialogue with the world religions.

The unity of the Christian churches (the abolition of all reciprocal excommunications) is necessary; peace between the religions (as the presupposition for a peace between the nations) is possible. But a maximum degree of ecumenical openness does not exclude loyalty to one's own religious conviction. Readiness for dialogue in steadfastness is desirable.

Forty years of theological work have gone into this book. The convictions which have grown in me through indefatigable study and reflection will be presented here briefly. The truth will always be spoken in truthfulness, and historical criticism will not be given up in favour of a psychologism reduced to the limits of the individual. Of course it was impossible in this small book to consider all aspects of Christian faith and life, from all the special questions of dogmatics to questions of ethics and spirituality. That is not least a consequence of the 'creed' itself, which presents a limited 'selection' from the possible 'articles' of Christian faith and does not go into questions of Christian action at all. Once this would have probably been called a 'Little Catechism' of Christian belief.

So for all the questions mentioned which I have not been able to discuss here I must refer the reader to my larger books which form the background to this small volume, above all *Justification*, *The Church*, *On Being A Christian*, *Does God Exist?*, *Eternal Life?*, *Christianity and the World Religions* and *Global Responsibility*. At the end – as evidence, and possibly to take the reader further – I have included a separate list of these works, which contain detailed bibliographies. I hope to go into the historical development of church and dogma and the present situation of Christianity in the second volume of my trilogy 'The Religious Situation of Our Time', the volume on Christianity, in the style that I adopted in *Judaism*, which appeared in German in 1991 and in English in 1992.

Although the 'Creed' has unmistakable limitations in content, because it was composed in the first half of the first millennium I felt it a greater challenge to tackle the traditional formulations of faith than to reformulate a modern confession of faith in my own words; no one can be interested in a completely diffuse, even confused piety. And it is these very articles which have put a deep stamp on Christianity – not least through their use in liturgy and church music down to the present day – and have even gone so far as to influence the graphic arts. For that reason, this time I have paid particular attention to the graphic arts, having reflected on the musical shaping of traditional statements of faith in connection with the name of Mozart. In each of the six chapters which follow I have tried to introduce the particular articles of faith with a classic example of Christian iconography in order to be able to compare the picture of traditional faith with the very different basic attitude of today's contemporaries.

In conclusion, I owe a word of thanks for the help which I have also received this time. That is anything but a formality for me.

For I am very aware that I could not cope with my enormous burden of work without reliable technical and scientific support. This time once again the technical production of the manuscript lay in the hands of Frau Eleonore Henn and Frau Margarita Krause; my doctoral student Matthias Schnell and Michel Hofmann have read the proofs carefully. Once again Stephan Schlensog has designed and set the book, and he was also a help to me in his critical reading of the typescript. For all questions of content and style, though, I am particularly grateful to Frau Marianne Saur and the Acting Director of the Institute for Ecumenical Research, Dr Karl-Josef Kuschel. I would like to express my gratitude quite publicly, with all my heart, to all of these who have stood faithfully by my side for so many years.

The one conviction behind this exposition of the Apostles' Creed is that even as a contemporary of the end of the twentieth century, despite all the criticism of Christianity and the church, one can say 'Credo, I believe', in an attitude of reasonable trust. I can say yes to the articles of the Apostles' Creed (which are certainly of very differing importance) as guidelines for my own living and hope for my own dying.

Tübingen, May 1992   Hans Küng

Symbolum Apostolorum

Credo in Deum Patrem omnipotentem
creatorem coeli et terrae.

Et in Iesum Christum
Filium eius unicum, dominum nostrum
qui conceptus est de Spiritu Sancto
natus ex Maria Virgine

passus sub Pontio Pilato
crucifixus, mortuus et sepultus

descendit ad infernos
tertia die resurrexit a mortuis
ascendit ad coelos
sedet ad dexteram Dei Patris omnipotentis
inde venturus est
iudicare vivos et mortuos.

Credo in Spiritum Sanctum
sanctam Ecclesiam catholicam
sanctorum communionem

remissionem peccatorum
carnis resurrectionem
et vitam eternam

Amen

The Apostles' Creed

I believe in God, the Father, the almighty,
creator of heaven and earth.

And in Jesus Christ,
his only Son, our Lord,
conceived by the Holy Spirit,
born of the Virgin Mary,

suffered under Pontius Pilate,
crucified, dead and buried,

descended into the realm of death,
on the third day risen from the dead,
ascended into heaven;
he is seated at the right hand of God, the almighty Father;
from there he will come
to judge the living and the dead.

I believe in the Holy Spirit,
the holy catholic church,
communion of saints,

forgiveness of sins,
resurrection of the dead
and eternal life.

Amen

I

God the Father: The Image of God and the Creation of the World

In six chapters, clearly divided, I want to attempt to show how we can understand the twelve articles of the traditional Creed. It is a creed which certainly does not go back to the apostles, but is inspired by the apostolic message. Only around 400 do the name *Symbolum Apostolorum* and the story of its apostolic origin appear. The Creed is found in its complete form only in the fifth century, and only in the tenth century was it introduced as a baptismal creed by Emperor Otto the Great in Rome in place of the Niceno-Constantinopolitan Creed. But it has held its place down to the present day in both the Catholic Church and the churches of the Reformation as a simple narrative summary of Christian faith on the basis of the apostolic preaching. So it also has an important ecumenical function. And yet any contemporary will immediately tend to ask, 'Can we believe it all?'

1. Can we believe it all?

The old baptismal question was put directly and personally: 'Do you believe in God, the Father, the almighty, the creator of heaven and earth?' This very first statement of the Creed already asks us 'to believe' a great deal. 'God' – 'Father' – 'almighty' – 'creator' – 'heaven and earth'. None of these words is obvious any longer. Each of them needs an explanation, a translation for our time.

Now people certainly do not live by concepts and ideas alone, but by the image that they have taken deep into themselves since their youth. Nor does human faith live only by statements, dogmas and arguments, but by any great image which has impressed itself as a truth of faith and can address itself not only to intellect and critical rational discourse but also to our power of imagination and our emotions. Faith would only be half a thing were it to address only our understanding and reason and not the whole person, including our hearts.

Moreover, for many contemporaries the word God, creator God, is less a concept or a definition than a picture, a great classical picture of God and the world, God and humankind. Like those frescoes which Michelangelo Buonarotti, barely thirty-five at the time, having previously worked almost exclusively as a sculptor and architect, painted on the giant vault of the chapel of the papal palace on the commission of Pope Julius II della Rovere between 1508 and 1512. Here we have unique pictures: unique not only because of their unprecedentedly concentrated overall artistic conception, the pseudo-architecture which supports the whole, the bold perspectives and the monumental character of the figures, and the shining colours which have now once again been restored, but unique also by virtue of their theological content. Instead of the apostles on lofty thrones in a work of painted geometrical fields, which is what the pope wanted, Michelangelo himself wanted to depict the story of creation and the primal history of humankind.

The result was quite unprecedented. Whereas the early Christian painters had contented themselves with depicting God by ciphers and symbols, Michelangelo ventured something which no one before him had attempted: to make the process of creation and the event of the very first day of creation directly visible:

God the Father hovering in empty space and dividing the light from the darkness with powerful gestures of his arms.

Then, on the second giant fresco, God as creator, storming in, creating the sun and moon in a moment, so that on the same picture we can see him from the back, flying away.

Further – after the division of the land from the water in the fourth central picture (all his life Michelangelo was never interested in plants and animals) – there is God the Father flying in, bringing the attractive, adolescent figure of Eve with him in an angel chariot. From God's right index figure the spark of life leaps over to Adam's hand, stretched out powerlessly to receive it.

No one had dared to paint such pictures beforehand, nor has anyone afterwards: they remain unsurpassed. And yet here immediately the sceptical contemporary will ask questions: 'Is this what we are to believe? Above all, those legendary stories in the Bible of a work of creation in six days, of a God up there on high, a superman and superfather, utterly male in form and almighty as well! Doesn't the Creed require us to abandon critical thought as we enter the church?'

Granted, we no longer live in the time of Michelangelo, who moroever more than anyone else in his later years relativized art in favour of religion. Nor do we live any longer in the times of Luther and Melanchthon, who by then had in their hands the truly revolutionary book of the Catholic dean Nicholas Copernicus about a heliocentric world system and rejected it – because it clearly contradicted the Bible – though without putting Copernicus on trial as the popes later tried Galileo. Around 400 years after Copernicus and 300 years after Galileo, 200 years after Kant and 100 years after Darwin (all initially condemned by a Roman 'teaching office' incapable of learning), I am aware that literally every word of the 'Apostles' Creed' must be translated into the post-Copernican, post-Kantian, indeed post-Darwinian and post-Einsteinian world, just as former generations, too, had to understand the same creed anew at decisive shifts of historical epoch: the early Middle Ages, the Reformation, the Enlightenment. And unfortunately, over the course of centuries every word of this creed – beginning with the words 'I believe' and 'God' – has been misunderstood, misused, even desecrated.

But are we for that reason to throw away these words of the Creed – put them on the rubbish heap of history? No! Bit by bit we have to re-lay the theological foundations and take the sceptical questions of contemporaries with the utmost seriousness. For the creed all too obviously presupposes things which in the conditions of modernity have to be proved: that there is a transcendent reality at all, that God exists. But prove? Does 'believe' mean prove?

2. What does 'believe' mean?

Granted, statements of faith do not have the character of mathematical or physical laws. Their content cannot be demonstrated as in mathematics or in physics by direct evidence or by an experiment that can be seen. But the reality of God would in no way be God's reality were it so visible, tangible, empirically detectable; if it could be verified by experiments or deduced by mathematical logic. 'A God who is there, is not God', as the Protestant theologian and resistance fighter Dietrich Bonhoeffer once rightly said. For God – understood most deeply and ultimately – cannot be simply an object. If God is that, that would not be God. God would then be the idol of human beings. God would be an entity among entities, at the disposal of human beings, even if only in their knowing him.

God is by definition that which cannot be defined, that which cannot be limited: a literally invisible, unfathomable, incomprehensible, infinite reality. Indeed, God is not some further dimension of our multi-dimensional reality, but is the dimension of infinity which is hiddenly present in all our everyday calculation, even if we do not perceive it – except in infinitesimal calculus, which as we know is part of higher mathematics.

The not only mathematical but real dimension of infinity, this sphere of the intangible and incomprehensible, this invisible and unfathomable reality of God, cannot be proved rationally, however much theologians and sometimes even scientists have kept trying to do so – in contrast to the Hebrew Bible, in contrast to the New Testament and in contrast to the Qur'an, where the existence of God is nowhere demonstrated by argument. From a philosophical point of view Immanuel Kant was right: our pure, theoretical reason does not reach this far. Bound to space and time, it cannot prove what is outside the horizon of our experience in space and time: either that God still exists or – and most atheists fail to see this – that God does not exist. So far no one has produced a convincing proof for the non-existence of God either. It is impossible to prove not only the existence of God but also the existence of a Nothingness.

Therefore no one is compelled on purely intellectual and philosophical grounds to accept the existence of God. Anyone who wants to accept the existence of a meta-empirical reality 'God' has no alternative but to get involved with it quite practically. For Kant, too, the existence of God is a postulate of practical reason. I would prefer to speak of an act of the human being as a whole, the human being with reason (Descartes!) and a heart (Pascal!); or, more precisely, an act of reasonable trust for which there may be no strict proofs, but for which there are good reasons. It's like committing oneself to someone else in love after some doubts; strictly speaking one has no strict proofs for this trust, but one does have good reasons – as long as this is not a fatal 'blind love'. And blind faith can have as devastating consequences as blind love.

So to this extent human faith in God is neither rational proof nor an irrational feeling nor a decisionistic act of the will, but a well-founded and in this sense a reasonable trust. In biblical terms, this reasonable trust, which includes thought, questioning and doubts, and is at the same time a matter of understanding, will and disposition, is called 'faith'. So it is not just a matter of holding statements to be true, but a commitment of the whole person, not primarily to specific statements, but to the very reality of God. Augustine of Hippo, the great teacher of the Latin church, already made a distinction: it is not just a matter of 'believing something' (*credere aliquid*) or even of 'believing someone' (*credere alicui*) but of 'believing in someone' (*credere in aliquem*). That is the meaning of the primal word '*Credo*', 'I believe':
– not in the Bible (which I say against Protestant biblicism), but in the one to whom the Bible bears witness;
– not in the tradition (which I say against Eastern Orthodox traditionalism), but in the one whom the tradition hands down;
– not in the church (which I say against Roman Catholic authoritarianism), but in the one whom the church proclaims;
so, and that is our ecumenical confession: '*Credo in Deum*', 'I believe in God'.

Even the Creed is not faith itself, but is merely an expression, formulation, articulation of faith; so we speak of 'articles of faith'. And yet a contemporary may ask me: 'Don't those who still believe in God go back on the Enlightenment? Aren't they willy-nilly falling back into the Middle Ages or at least the time of the

Reformation? Isn't this utterly to forget, indeed to suppress, the whole criticism of religion in modern times?'

3. Does the modern criticism of religion still hold?

No, I have not forgotten the criticism of religion; I have studied it for years, with much passion and truly not without sympathy for the great figures of this genre, from Feuerbach through Marx to Nietzsche and Freud. In all too many things they were and are right, so that even today (or again today) we ignore them at our peril. For if we analyse the profile of the personalities of so many pious 'believers' – not just in Christianity – we cannot dispute Ludwig Feuerbach's view that belief in God can alienate people from themselves and warp them because they have adorned God with the treasures of their own inner depths. These believers are not human enough, not human beings enough, for the godless to be infected by their belief in God. Indeed we can understand how the republican Feuerbach wanted to change people from being candidates for the beyond into students of this world; from being religious and political servants of the heavenly and earthly monarchy and aristocracy to being free citizens with an awareness of themselves.

However, since Feuerbach we have learned two things:

1. Feuerbach never proved, but only asserted, that God is merely a hypostatized reflection of man, projected on to the beyond, behind whom there is nothing in reality. Today there are countless people who are free citizens of the earth, fully aware of themselves, precisely because they believe in God as the ground and guarantee of their freedom and coming of age.

2. Godless humanism, too, has all too often had inhuman consequences, and in the experiences of terror in our century – two world wars, the Gulag, the Holocaust, the atom bomb – the way from humanity without divinity to bestiality has often proved a short one.

But, it may be asked, doesn't this statement about free people with an awareness of themselves who believe in God apply at best to prosperous Western countries, but hardly to continents like Latin America? Haven't people there rightly applied insights from Karl Marx to the analysis of the inhumane conditions for which not least religion and the church are responsible? Marx wanted to turn the criticism of heaven into the criticism of the earth, the criticism of religion into the criticism of law, the criticism of theology into the criticism of politics. Anyone who knows the often inhumane conditions in, say, Latin America can hardly dispute that the ruler God of the Christians was often the God of the rulers: a consolation for the world to come, a disfigurement of the consciousness, a flowery decoration for the chains when they should have been broken.

Meanwhile, however, it has also been demonstrated even to those who so far have proved unteachable that despite all the correct analyses the Marxist solutions – abolition of private property and socialization of industry, agriculture, education and culture – have led to an unprecedented exploitation of the peoples and a destruction of morality and nature. But globally speaking, religion did not automatically die out, as Marx assumed. Instead of religion, for a while revolution was the opium of the people – from the Elbe to Vladivostok, and also in Cuba, in Vietnam, Cambodia and China. But now from Eastern Europe and East Germany through South Africa to South America and the Philippines it has proved that religion can be not only a means of social appeasement and consolation but also – as already in the North American civil rights movement – a catalyst of social liberation: and this without that revolutionary use of force which results in a vicious circle of ever-new violence.

'Granted,' some contemporary may say, 'belief in God may be a catalyst for external, social liberation. But what about the even more urgent inner, psychological liberation from anxiety, immaturity and a lack of freedom?' I concede that Sigmund Freud quite rightly criticized the churches' arrogance and misuse of power; he criticized the false forms of religion, blindness to reality, self-deception, attempts at flight and repression of sexuality; but he also criticized quite directly the traditional authoritarian image of God. In fact behind the ambivalence of this image of God it is possible to see the image of a person's own father or mother in early childhood projected into a metaphysical dimension, the beyond or the future. And even today in religious families the penal Father-God is sometimes misused by parents as an instrument for training or disciplining their children, with long-term negative consequences for the religion of adolescents. So belief in God seems to be a return to infantile structures, a regression to childish wishes.

In the meantime, however, it has proved,
– that not only sexuality but also religious feeling can be repressed;
– that the oldest, strongest, most urgent wishes of humankind, which according to Freud are the strength of religion, are better not dismissed as sheer illusions!
– that in a time of general lack of orientation and often meaninglessness, belief in God in particular can help to give living and indeed dying a definitive meaning, and also to provide unconditional ethical criteria and a spiritual home.

So belief in God, not least in the psychological sphere, can have a liberating rather than an enslaving function, a healing rather than a damaging function, a truly stabilizing rather than a destabilizing function.

This may have made it clear that those who believe in God – first of all generally described as a transcendent-immanent, all-embracing all-permeating utterly real reality in human beings and the world – need not fall back either into the Middle Ages or into the time of the Reformation, or into their own childhood, but can be real contemporaries among contemporaries, today in particular, in the painfully slow transition to a post-modern epoch of the world.

So to sum up my answer to the modern criticism of religion:
– Belief in God was and certainly often is authoritarian, tyrannical and reactionary. It can produce anxiety, immaturity, narrow-mindedness, intolerance, injustice, frustration and social isolation; it can even legitimate and inspire immorality, social abuse and wars within a nation or between nations. But:
– Particularly in recent decades belief in God has again been able to show itself increasingly to be liberating, orientated on the future and beneficial to human beings: belief in God can spread trust in life, maturity, broad-mindedness, tolerance, solidarity, creative and social commitment; it can further spiritual renewal, social reform and world peace.

'But what about the specific statements of our Christian creed? How are we to understand, under the conditions of the modern criticism of religion, that God is the "creator" of heaven and earth? Don't the insights of modern cosmology contradict belief in a creator?' These are the questions of many contemporaries.

4. Belief in creation and cosmology – a contradiction?

'In the beginning, God created heaven and earth' – that is the very first statement of the Bible. So this world had a beginning, set by an act of God. Many natural scientists today also assume that the world is not eternal, without a beginning, but had a beginning in time, which possibly coincided with a Big Bang. But I can immediately hear the objection: 'Are you seeking scientific verification for what the Bible says about a divine creation of the world? Do you see the moment of the Big Bang with which distinguished scientists think our world began as identical with the moment of the creation of the world from nothing by divine omnipotence?'

The cosmological 'standard model' (as S. Weinberg calls it) of the origin of the world which was developed on the basis of the Big Bang theory has very recently found amazing confirmation. As early as 1929 the American physicist Edwin P. Hubble concluded from the red shifts of the spectrum lines of galaxies (Milky Way systems) which he discovered that our universe is still expanding. With a speed which is proportional to their distance from us, in this view the galaxies outside our own Milky Way are moving away from us. Since when? It cannot have been from eternity. There must have been a beginning in which all radiation and all matter was compressed into an almost indescribable primal fireball of infinitesimal size and the utmost density and heat. The uniform (and isotropic) expansion of the universe which is still going on is said to have begun with a gigantic cosmic explosion, the Big Bang – at a temperature of 100 billion degrees Celsius and with a density around 4 billion times that of water – almost 15 billion years ago.

In the very first seconds particles, both heavy (protons and neutrons) and light (electrons, positrons), the elements of atoms, will have been formed from photons extremely rich in energy. Afterwards, nuclei of helium will have formed by nuclear processes from protons and neutrons, and again, some hundred thousand years later, atoms of hydrogen and helium will also have been constructed. Only very much later – as the pressure of the originally high-energy quanta of light decreased and there was further cooling – could the gas condense through gravitation into clusters, and finally, after further gradual condensation, into galaxies and stars. The radiation in the decimetre and centimetre sphere (cosmic microwaves or background radiation) discovered in 1964 by A.A.Penrose and R.W.Wilson was thus simply the remains of that very hot cosmic radiation associated with the Big Bang which through the expansion of the universe became a radiation of very low temperature, as it were a Big Bang echo. In April 1992 it proved possible for the first time, with the help of the US research satellite COBE, to measure the traces of those tiny and earliest structures in the space-time structure which were caused by the first process of explosion and from which finally the galaxies formed: the greatest and oldest structures (variations of density in the early cosmic soup of energy) which came into being 300,000 years after the Big Bang.

So was Michelangelo so utterly wrong? And isn't the Bible right: 'And God said, Let there be light! And there was light. And God saw that the light was good . . . a first day' (Gen.1.3f.). Doesn't the Big Bang theory clearly prove the truth of a creation of the world? Doesn't this sudden act of creation have something of the character of a Big Bang, infinitely more grandiose than the biblical writers and even Michelangelo could have imagined in their time? According to that theory the Big Bang certainly took place a long time ago, but in finite time. So the world would have a beginning, a specific age – around 15 billion years. So would our planet, formed from cosmic dust-clouds on the periphery of one of the hundred million Milky Way systems formed five billion years ago. Indeed, the most recent measurements put the age of the solar system, which came into being from a condensing spiral cloud of gas and dust, from which our primal earth was also formed, at 4.5 billion years.[1]

But the snag about this theory is that it has still not been decided whether the expansion of the universe will go on permanently or whether it will come to a stop and then become a contraction. That can only be decided from further observations, on which it also depends whether the universe is open or closed, i.e. whether space is infinite or has a finite volume. As is well known, even before the Big Bang theory Albert Einstein developed a new model of the world, though it was then still static, which differed completely from the classical physics of Newton: on the basis of the equations of his general theory of relativity, gravity is seen as a consequence of a curvature in the invisible 'space-time-continuum', i.e. a four-dimensional sphere which is formed of co-ordinates of space and time by means of non-Euclidean geometry. This is a spatially curved universe which has to be thought of as unlimited yet has a finite volume – like the surface of a sphere in three-dimensional space, which has a finite surface and yet no limits.

Advocates of dialectical materialism condemned Einstein's model of a universe finite in space and time at a very early stage as 'idealistic', for reasons of belief; it seemed not to confirm their dogma of the infinity and eternity of matter. And when in apologetic Christian writings constant attempts were made in fact to identify the point of the Big Bang with a divine creation of the world, non-Marxist scientists were also disturbed. As the German astronomer Otto Heckmann put it: 'Some younger scientists were so upset by these theological tendencies that they resolved simply to block up their cosmological source. They created "steady state cosmology", the cosmology of the expanding but unchanging universe.'[2] But this theory of a stationary universe presupposed a spontaneous production of matter and appeared contradictory; and after the discovery of cosmic microwave radiation, and also of quasars and pulsars in the 1960s, it has virtually no prospect of establishing itself.

But I hear the sceptic asking: 'So do you really want to claim scientific confirmation for biblical statements about a creation of the world by God?' No, I don't want to do that. Scientists rightly accuse theologians of having all too often used God to fill in the cosmic gaps, to explain what has so far been inexplicable, and of having thus made their contribution to the 'need for a home for God' which was pointed out by the zoologist Ernst Haeckel at the turn of the century. Indeed, doesn't God become more dispensable with every new scientific explanation and then, as the English philosopher Antony Flew pointed out, die the death of a thousand qualifications? And are believers to withdraw to that remnant of the world which has not yet been explained, as a base for demonstrating a creator? No, the theologian may not make the truth of belief in the creation of the world depend on the chance state of particle physics or molecular biology.

Conversely, however, philosophers or natural scientists – with a Nobel prize here or there – may not seek to prove their atheistic standpoint (which they have a complete right to present) with the results of physics or biology. Here there is a risk of their exceeding their competence; indeed, here the limits of pure reason laid down by Kant are transgressed. We must remember that nuclear physics and astrophysics aren't yet in a position to solve quite basic riddles of origins (as is shown by *Origins* – a collection of interviews with leading cosmologists published in 1990[3]) and perhaps will never be able to do so. Why doesn't the cosmos begin with a chaos, but with a primal state of amazing order? Why are all the constants of nature (e.g. the velocity of light) and quite specific natural laws to which we owe energy and matter, and also space and time, there from the Big Bang on? Why do the same physical conditions (temperature?) prevail everywhere in the cosmos? Why isn't the cosmos again lapsing into chaos from a state of relative order, in accordance with the physical law of entropy?

Instead of being annoyed that they cannot explain the moment of creation itself (as it were the first billionth of a second), scientists would do better to put quite rationally the question: What was 'before' the Big Bang? Or more precisely, what was the condition for the possibility of the Big Bang – in terms of energy and matter, space and time? Here, however, the cosmological question becomes the theological question, beyond the limits of pure reason, and even for cosmologists it becomes the great question of trust. So once again the question, which can now be answered constructively:

5. Can we believe in the creator God in the age of cosmology?

The question about the first creative ground of grounds whom we call God, the creator God, is not just the question of a singular event at the beginning. This is also the question of the fundamental relationship between the world and God generally. Creation goes on; God's creative action goes on! And only if we bid farewell to outdated modern ideas of a 'God without a home' or a 'meaningless universe' can we have some inkling of the magnitude of an ongoing creation, a *creatio continua*. But in connection with the beginning of the world as reported by the Bible and presupposed by the Creed, I can now sum up my answer in a few sentences like this, backed up by contemporary biblical exegesis:

1. That our universe is possibly finite in space and time (from a scientific perspective) is of considerable significance for our understanding of ourselves and God; it confirms the insight into the finitude of all that is. But the reverse is also the case: even an infinite universe could not limit the infinite God, who is indeed in all things. That means that belief in God is compatible with a variety of models of the world. And the theological apologists are as much on the wrong track as their anti-theological opponents.

2. However, the question of the ultimate origin of the world and human beings – what was before the Big Bang and hydrogen? – remains a question which human beings cannot dismiss. It leads directly to what (according to Leibniz and Heidegger) is the basic question of philosophy: why is there anything and not nothing? Scientists, who have no competence beyond the horizon of experience, cannot answer it; but they may not dismiss it as useless and even meaningless because it is a burden to them (and often also to philosophers). Who has demonstrated that the question of the meaning of the whole is meaningless?

3. The language of the Bible is not a scientific language of facts but a metaphorical picture language. The Bible does not seek to state any scientific facts; it seeks to interpret them. The two biblical accounts of creation, the first written around 900 and the second around 500 BCE, give no information about the origin of the universe in the modern scientific sense. But they do give a testimony of faith as to its ultimate origin, which natural science can neither confirm nor refute. And this testimony runs: at the beginning of the world there is not chance and arbitrariness, a demon or blind energy, but *God*, God's good purpose for creation. This God does not need to be understood either as the great architect or as the clever watchmaker who puts things together perfectly from outside and determines their order completely.

4. That God made the world 'out of nothing' is not a scientific statement about a 'false vacuum' with 'negative gravity', nor is it

the becoming independent of Nothingness (as it were a black void) before or alongside God; it is a theological expression for the fact that the world and human beings along with space and time owe themselves to God alone and to no other cause.

5. The testimony of faith of the biblical accounts of creation, like Michelangelo's frescoes, answers in images and similes questions which are also unavoidable for people today and which science with its method and language cannot answer. And this is the message of the first page of the Bible:
- The good God is the origin of each and every one.
- God is not in competition with any evil or demonic counter-principle.
- The world as a whole and in detail, including night, matter, even lowly creatures, the human body and sexuality are fundamentally good.
- The creation of the good God already represents his gracious concern for the world and human beings.
- So human beings are the goal of the process of creation, and precisely for that reason they are responsible for the care of their environment, nature.

Thus it has become clear that to believe in the one God who made heaven and earth, indeed the whole universe, does not mean deciding for one or other model of the world, one or other theory of the cosmos (they may be right or wrong). When we talk of God we are concerned with the presupposition of all models of the world and the world generally. To believe in God, the creator of heaven and earth, does not therefore mean believing in some myths of primal times, nor does it mean believing that God is creator as Michelangelo painted him on the ceiling of the Sistine Chapel. Here all conceptions end. And pictures remain – pictures.

To believe in the creator of the world means to affirm in enlightened trust that the ultimate origin of the world and human beings does not remain inexplicable, that the world and human beings are not hurled meaninglessly from nothingness to nothingness, but that as a whole they are meaningful and valuable – not just chaos, but cosmos; because they have a first and last security in God as their primal ground, primal author, creator. And this decisive notion is also expressed in the pictures of the great Michelangelo. So with respect to the beginning of all beginnings, the origin of all origins, because here we are concerned with *God* we may use that term 'mystery', often misused by theologians for whatever runs contrary to reason: as Eberhard Jüngel has put it, *God as the Mystery of the World.*

But here it is important that nothing should compel us to this faith. We can decide on it in all freedom. But once we have decided, then this belief changes our position in the world, changes our attitude to the world; it roots our basic trust in this reality which is so ambivalent and makes our trust in God specific. And yet this question about God the creator and evolver needs an even more basic answer – particularly given the most recent results of biology. The question which is important for contemporaries cannot be avoided: 'What about the origin of life?'

6. The transition to life – an intervention by the creator God?

God, human beings and the world must be seen today against the background of evolution – scholastic theology may have outwardly resolved the dispute with the natural sciences but did not settle it! As late as 1950, in the encyclical *Humani Generis*, Pius XII wanted to commit church and theology to the view that the whole of humanity emerged from a single human couple – of course so as to be able to maintain the biblical narrative of the Fall word for word. A perfect primal state – Fall – Redemption: three historical stages? As if here, too, we didn't have to distinguish between picture language, symbols, modes of expression and what is meant. As if the third chapter of the book of Genesis (the story of the Fall), too, did not have to be applied to human beings generally instead of merely to a first human couple. As if there had ever been a world without desire and death, devouring and being devoured.

We shall be discussing later the substance of the story, the way in which all human beings are caught up in guilt and sin. But the idea of an 'original sin'[4] handed down by sexual procreation – which does not appear either in the Hebrew Bible or in the New Testament, but was propagated by the church father Augustine (and because of which the newborn had to be baptized!) – can no longer be maintained, because there never was this human couple who sinned for all humankind. The theologian and Teilhard specialist Karl Schmitz-Moormann is right in saying: 'The classical theory of redemption is imprisoned in a static view of the world in which to begin with everything was good, and in which evil first came into the world through human beings. The notion of this traditional view of redemption as reconciliation and ransom from the consequences of Adam's fall is nonsense for anyone who knows about the evolutionary background to human existence in the modern world.'[5]

However, many contemporaries have fewer difficulties with the biblical creation story, the works of the six days (now largely understood metaphorically), than with the subsequent history of salvation and the biblical miracle stories (at which Michelangelo only hints). Their difficulties are: 'Isn't the history of the world from beginning to end a consecutive, consistent development in which everything comes under the law of cause and effect (within this world) and each step clearly follows from the one before? So how can there still be room for a special "intervention" of God?'

Now the biology of recent decades has had such sensational success, particularly in connection with the origin of life, that today we may take it that Darwin's theory of evolution has been justified and tested experimentally in physics not only at the level of the living cell, but also at that of the molecule – by molecular biology, which, since the middle of the century, has come to represent something like the new basis for biology. Darwin had already expressed the hope that one day the principle of life would be recognized as a part or consequence of a quite general law. But what seemed a dream only a few decades ago has become a reality: the molecular biology of our days seems to have discovered this law. Biology has been revolutionized by it, just as a little earlier physics was revolutionized by quantum mechanics.

We now know that the elementary vehicles of life are two classes of macromolecules, nucleic acids and proteins. The chain molecules of the nucleic acids (DNA, RNA), principally in cell nuclei, form the central control. They contain in sequence the complete blueprint for the construction and functioning of any living being in coded form (according to a 'genetic code' which consists of only four 'characters') and hand it down from cell to cell, from generation to generation. The proteins (many-sided structures made up of amino-acids) take over this 'information'.

They carry out the functions of the living cell transferred to them by these instructions for construction and functioning. In this way life functions and propagates itself: a wonderful world at the most basic level, where in the smallest conceivable space molecules make their moves often in a millionth of a second.

But however we explain the transition to life in detail, it rests on a self-organization of matter, the molecule. For that is the basis for the 'ascent' in evolution from primitive forms to ever-higher forms, which it is better to call the ascendance theory rather than the descendance theory: already at the level of the molecule the principle of 'natural selection' and 'survival of the fittest', first established by Darwin in the world of plants and animals, prevails, a principle which inexorably forces development upwards at the cost of the less fit molecules. According to these most recent results of biophysics, it is hard to see how, given matter which organizes itself, a self-regulating evolution, there was any need for a special intervention by the creator God. On existing material presuppositions the origin of life is an event which runs its course completely by internal laws: the transition from inanimate to animate took place continuously or, to be precise, almost continuously.

Here we find the same problem as in quantum mechanics: an indeterminacy, a lack of sharpness, fortuitousness in the individual processes. Moreover we note a remarkable ambivalence: the overall course of biological evolution is determined, guided by laws, necessary. But often the higher development stood at a crossroads, and often nature took both ways – e.g. towards both insects and mammals. That means that individual events in their temporal sequence are undetermined, 'chance'. In other words, the ways which evolution takes in detail cannot be established in advance. The abrupt, microscopically small hereditary changes (mutations) from which sudden alterations and new phenomena also appear in the macroscopic sphere by an avalanche of growth or overloading are fortuitous. Thus life develops by 'chance and necessity' (Democritus)! This was the title which the French molecular biologist and Nobel prizewinner Jacques Monod gave to his well-known book (1970), in which he decisively gave priority to chance: 'Pure chance, absolutely free but blind, blind freedom at the very root of the stupendous edifice of evolution.'[6] So is everything chance? And precisely for that reason, is there no need for a creator and sustainer of this structure, as Monod assumes?

In his 1975 book *The Game*, the German biophysicist Manfred Eigen, also a Nobel prizewinner, formulated the counter-thesis, largely shared by biologists today, with the sub-title: 'Natural laws guide chance'.[7] Or, as Eigen writes in the preface to the German edition of Monod's book: 'Much as the individual form owes its origin to chance, the process of selection and evolution is absolutely necessary. No more! So there is no mysterious inherent "vital property" of matter which is ultimately also to determine the course of history. But also no less – not just chance!'[8] So does God play dice? 'Certainly,' answers the Viennese biologist Rupert Riedl, taking up Eigen, 'but he also follows his own rules. And only the tension between the two gives us meaning and freedom at the same time.'[9] So both chance and necessity, indeterminacy and determination, indeed materialism and idealism, are false alternatives in the explanation of evolution.

Even 'chaos' theory – abstract sciences (and the media) love dramatic names – does not make much difference to this (since it too, of course, presupposes order). So precisely the same answer is to be given to the question which is the title of Ian Stewart's witty book, *Does God Play Dice?* However, what this British mathematician says gives food for thought. 'An infinitely intelligent being with perfect senses – God, Vast Intellect, or Deep Thought – might actually be able to predict exactly when a given atom of radium will decay, a given electron shift its orbit. But with our limited intellects and imperfect senses, we may never be able to find the trick.'[10]

But if God thus plays dice within rules, for our contemporaries the question still arises: 'Is it *God* playing dice here? Doesn't self-organizing matter, self-regulating evolution, make the assumption of God superfluous?'

7. Can we believe in the creator in the age of biology?

First of all a distinction has to be made:
– It is an unjustified assumption – and here Monod and other biologists would agree – to postulate the existence of God on the basis of the transition from the inanimate world to the biosphere

or even on the basis of molecular indeterminacy. This would again be the hapless God of the gaps.

– But it is also an unjustified assumption to rule out the existence of God on the basis of the evidence from molecular biology. Just as the natural sciences do not provide proof of God, so they do not postulate that human beings 'do not need belief in God'.

Therefore we can now also give a constructive answer to the question, 'Can we believe in a creator in the age of biology?' The biologist, like the cosmologist, is confronted with an existential alternative:

Either we say no to a primal ground, primal content and primal goal of the whole process of evolution; in which case we have to accept the meaninglessness of the whole process and take into account the total forsakenness of human beings in the cosmos and the biosphere, as Monod consistently did.

Or (like many biologists) we say yes to a primal ground, primal content and primal goal. While we may not be able to prove that the whole process is fundamentally meaningful, we may presuppose this meaning in trust. And the question of the mystery of matter, of energy, of evolution, indeed the question of the mystery of being ('Why is there something and not nothing?') would then be answered. For as the scientist Hoimar von Ditfurth says, 'The mystery is not *how* evolution takes place, but *that* it takes place . . . We are beginning to see how that happens. But our science must recognize its inadequacy when we ask why this development and its order exists at all.'[11]

However, we should avoid mixing up scientific knowledge and religious confessions: we will not follow Teilhard de Chardin in attributing to the evolutionary process itself the direction towards a particular Omega point, thus giving it a meaning in terms of ethical-religious impulses (laudable though these might be). Such meaning cannot be provided by science, but only by religious faith. I have argued for a yes to an 'Alpha' as the 'ground' of everything and will also argue for an 'Omega' as the 'goal' of everything. But it must remain clear that this is a 'yes beyond science'.

Now if that is clear, the answer to the question of the relationship between belief in the creator and the origin of life can only be the following.

1. In the view of leading biologists a direct supernatural intervention by God in the origin of life – and by analogy also in the origin of the human spirit – seems more than ever unnecessary. The process of evolution as such, from a scientific point of view, neither implies nor excludes a primal ground, a creator and guide (an Alpha) or an ultimate goal of meaning (an Omega).

2. But for biologists, too, as long as they acknowledge their humanity, the human existential question arises as to the primal ground, meaning and goal of the whole process. Where does this whole process come from and what is it for? Science is incapable of answering this question. It calls for an existential decision.

3. This decision is again a matter of reasonable trust: one assumes either an ultimate groundlessness, baselessness and meaninglessness, or a primal ground, primal base and primal meaning of everything: a creator, guide and perfecter of the evolutionary process. Only a yes in faith to a primal ground, primal base and primal meaning can answer the question of the origin, basis and goal of the evolutionary process and thus give people hope for an ultimate certainty and security.

This prepares us to answer the equally difficult question about particular attributes of God. For today this has also become a real question for many believers: 'Can we believe in God as a Father, an almighty?'

8. Can we believe in God the 'Father', the 'almighty'?

For a long time there have been widespread reservations about an 'almighty' who is directly responsible for everything, who then with the progress of modernity is at best understood as a miraculous helper in need with only limited competence. Indeed, who would not have reservations about a God who can be called on wherever in nature and history we can make no further progress with our human science and technology, economics and politics, or can no longer cope with our personal problems? That would be a God who with spiritual and material progress and the development of psychology would become increasingly dispensable intellectually and superfluous practically, and therefore increasingly incredible.

But I also grant that after Auschwitz, the Gulag and two world wars it is even more difficult for me to speak boldly of 'God the almighty', who, 'de-tached' as 'ab-solute' power, untouched by all suffering, nevertheless guides everything in a detached way, brings about everything, or at least could do if he wanted to, and yet does not intervene in the greatest natural catastrophes and crimes of humanity, but keeps silent and keeps silent and keeps silent . . .

'Almighty' (Greek *pantocrator* = 'ruler of all', Latin *omnipotens* = 'capable of doing everything'): this attribute does not primarily express God's creative power but his superiority and effectiveness, which is not opposed by any principle of a numinous or political kind independent of him. In the Greek translation of the Hebrew Bible the word is mostly used for Sabaoth (Lord of 'hosts'), but in the New Testament – apart from the book of Revelation (and one quotation in Paul) – it is strikingly avoided. However, in patristics this attribute of God then becomes an expression of the universal claim of Christianity in the name of the one God, and in scholasticism it is the object of much speculation about all that God can do and cannot do (because it is intrinsically impossible).

When modern constitutions are still proclaimed 'in the name of God, the almighty', not only is political power legitimated, but a limit is also set to the absolutizing of human power. Only enlightened faith in God is an ultimately well-founded answer to what Horst Eberhard Richter calls the 'God-complex', the human delusion of omnipotence. However, in the Creed (and in many official prayers), in the light of the New Testament one would without doubt prefer other more frequent and more 'Christian' attributes to the predicate 'almighty': 'all gracious' or also (as in the Qur'an) 'all merciful' God. Or – if the word were not so completely worn out – simply 'dear God', as an expression of what from a Christian perspective might be the deepest description of God, 'God is love' (I John 4.8,16).

Later we shall have to go into the question of God and human suffering. But after all that we have already heard, we may not begin in mediaeval or even Reformation fashion from a God 'over' or 'outside' the world:

1. If under the conditions of modernity (Hegel and the consequences) God is to be thought of in the light of a modern unitary

understanding of reality, then God can only be thought of in the world and the world in God, and God's activity in the world cannot be understood as being finite and relative, but only as the infinite in the finite and the absolute in the relative. So:

2. God, then, does not work into the world from above or outside as the unmoved mover, as an architect or watchmaker, but works from within as the most real dynamic reality in the process of the development of the world. God makes this possible, permeates it and completes it. God does not work above the world process but in the world process: in, with and among human beings and things. God is origin, centre and goal of the world process.

3. God is not just active at individual, particularly important, points or gaps in the world process, but works as the creative and perfect primal basis and thus as the guide of the world, immanent in it and superior to it, while fully respecting the laws of nature, which have their origin in God. God is the all-embracing and all permeating ground of meaning of the world process, who can of course only be accepted in faith.

But if I know all that, then may I not perhaps in a restrained way also again speak in what Paul Ricoeur calls a 'second naivety' of God, the 'Father in heaven'? May I not look upwards, to the firmament, to heaven, which in its infinity, clarity and beauty was always the real symbol for God, and can continue to be today, particularly for those trained in science? For I know that God as understood today is not a human being, a person as we are, but infinitely more than a person. But in such a way that God does not simply become an abstract apersonal principle, impersonal, less than a person. Rather, God is trans-personal, supra-personal: the infinite itself in all that is finite, pure spirit. God, the infinite and ungraspable, is the sea which (*pace* Nietzsche's 'madman') is not drunk up; is the horizon which cannot be swept away; is the sun from which the earth and human beings cannot be detached.

But if I thus know that God is the all-embracing, all-permeating, infinite reality, which must not be thought of as separate from my finitude but as different from it, then I can recognize that it is not meaningless also to recognize this all-embracing spiritual reality as something over against me, indeed to address this overarching, grounding 'over against' who is outside or within me. Then I can say 'You' to God, to this Infinite which embraces me, and can again – as people of all continents have done over the millennia of the Jewish-Christian-Islamic tradition – pray: praising and often lamenting, giving thanks, asking and sometimes also rebelling in fury.

'But God as Father – an utterly male figure?' Here too, prompted by the contribution of feminist theologians, I know better than I did that this God is not male, that God is neither masculine nor feminine, that God transcends masculinity and femininity, that all our terms for God, including the word 'Father', are only analogies and metaphors, only symbols and ciphers, and that none 'fixes' the symbol God, so that one might, say, obstruct women's liberation in society and the ordination of women in the church in the name of such a patriarchal God.

But if I thus know that God is the unspeakable mystery of our reality, who embraces and positively transcends and does away with all the oppositions of the world, including that of gender (what Nicholas of Cusa called the *coincidentia oppositorum*, the coincidence of opposites), then, as we human beings now have no higher names than human names, and 'father' or 'mother' say more to us than 'the Absolute' or 'Being itself', we can again pray quite simply and at the same time post-patriarchally – thus including God's motherhood – in the way that Jesus taught us almost two thousand years ago: 'Our Father'.

But today many contemporaries are asking, 'Must what Christians may believe from the scriptures of the Old Testament (God as Creator) and New Testament (God as Father who cares for his creation) be so completely different from what other religions have learned from their masters?' The answer to this is, 'No', so at the end of this first chapter, here is an important inter-religious survey.

9. *The common belief in God of the three prophetic religions*

The understanding of God and creation which I have developed here is not just valid for Christianity. Judaism and Islam also believe in God, the Almighty, the Creator of heaven and earth. Indeed, as we well know, Judaism, Christianity and Islam are the three prophetic religions which believe in one and the same God of Abraham.

Even more important than their derivation from the same Near Eastern region and the same semitic language-group is the common belief shared by Judaism, Christianity and Islam:

– belief in one and the same God of Abraham, their tribal ancestor, who according to all three traditions was the great witness of this one true and living God;

– a view of history which does not think in cosmic cycles but is directed towards a goal: a universal history of salvation progressing from the beginning in God's creation through time, for individual human beings, too, focussed on an end brought about by God's consummation;

– the prophetic proclamation and the revelation laid down once for all in the Holy Scriptures, which remains normative;

– the basic ethic of an elemental humanity grounded in belief in the one God: the ten 'words' or commandments (or their equivalent) as an expression of God's will. Here we have a nucleus, a basic element for a common world ethic of the world religions for which parallels can also be found in the other religions.

In a word: Judaism, Christianity and Islam, these three Abrahamic religions, together form an ethically orientated monotheistic world movement of Near-Eastern, Semitic origin and prophetic character. A common commitment of these three religions to peace, justice and freedom, to human dignity and human rights, without any of the religious fanaticism which constantly threatens, is urgent, particularly in the face of intensified fundamentalist trends in all three religions.

But here of course – and I am only mentioning this in passing – the religions of Indian and Chinese origin must also be included. For they too believe in an absolute, in an ultimate, supreme reality: Brahman in the Hindu tradition; Dharma, Dharmakaya or Nirvana in the Buddhist tradition; and Tao or T'ien/heaven in the Chinese tradition.

To develop what these religions in the three different river systems – of Semitic, Indian and Chinese origin – have in common and where they differ would belong in a systematic theology of world religions. In connection with this first article of faith it should simply be emphasized that we should not be deceived by the real or even merely apparent polytheism in the religions of the Indian and Chinese river systems. When Indians, Chinese or Japanese enter a Bavarian or Italian baroque church, they do not exactly gain the impression of a monotheistic religion. Conversely, all the different demonic and divine beings in India, China or Japan are completely different from the one ultimate Reality. The religions of Chinese and Indian origin also recognize and acknowledge an Ultimate, Supreme or Deepest that determines all reality, whether this is as a ruling or indwelling person or as a supreme and pervasive principle.

– Since earliest times Chinese religion has known two names for God: on the one hand 'Lord in the heights' (Shang-ti), the supreme ruler over all gods and spirits of nature, and on the other hand 'heaven' (T'ien), a cosmic, moral power (order, being) possessing intelligence and will, which directs the fate of all human beings impartially: both names are associated with the designation of the one supreme being, the all-embracing power. In Chinese Taoism Tao ('the way') stands for this ultimate transcendent reality.

– In the Hindu religions since the time of the Upanishads the one all-embracing Brahman is accepted as the ultimate reality to which human beings find access by way of mystical contemplation, despite the degree to which this belief is associated with a wealth of anthropomorphic, personalistic myths.

However, despite all that the religions have in common, the distinctions between them may not be swept aside, and there are essential differences even between the three prophetic religions which believe in the one God of Abraham. Judaism is concentrated on God's People and Land; Christianity on God's Messiah and Son; and Islam on God's Word and Book. But today we should not treat these differences in the demonic spirit of triumphalism and pious fanaticism but in the spirit of understanding and peace. And if in the following chapters I have to concentrate on what is specifically Christian, at the same time everything must be done to avoid even the slightest hint of anti-Judaism or anti-Islamism. I shall try to express what is specifically Christian in such a way that it does not deter Jews and Muslims, but invites them to find the way at least a little more comprehensible, and perhaps to go along it together one stage further.

It has already become clear that belief in the one God has consequences for ethics. In a transitional age like our own, in which many people (especially intellectuals and people in key positions) are infected by that 'universal diffuse cynicism', in a world in which so many values are worn out, so many convictions venal, in which faith seems to have sunk to being improvement and morality to have been replaced by a selfish perception of one's own interests, for humankind to survive it will be necessary to adopt and live out another, alternative basic ethical attitude. What will it be grounded in? As a human being, I have in reasonable trust in God an 'Archimedean point', a firm standpoint, from which I can at least determine, move and change 'my world', an absolute that I can hold on to. Free commitment to this one absolute gives me great freedom over against all that is relative in this world – no matter how important and powerful it may be. In the end I am responsible only to this God and not to the state or the church, to a party or a firm, to the pope or any leader. This belief in God is thus the anchorage for an alternative basic ethical attitude. As we shall see in the next chapter, its criterion is God's Word, its vitality his Spirit. But its centre is freedom and love and its focal point – perhaps also for some of our contemporaries – new hope and joy in life.

II

Jesus Christ: Virgin Birth and Divine Sonship

How can evolution (about which we have been talking so far) and incarnation (about which we shall be talking next) fit together? As has become increasingly clear in our century, evolution is a universal concept which embraces the whole reality of world, life and humanity, of cosmogenesis, biogenesis and anthropogenesis. To be specific:

– cosmogenesis: evolution does not just mean the history of biological development but the whole development of the cosmos, that world history which began with the Big Bang around fifteen billion years ago;

– biogenesis: the first forms of life also developed from the previous phases of development of inanimate matter, a process which microbiology has already largely been able to explain;

– anthropogenesis: even more, human beings have themselves developed from lower forms of life, albeit over enormously long periods of time, and will possibly continue to develop further unless they destroy themselves, so that present-day man is in no way already to be understood as the goal of the development, the pinnacle of evolution, the 'crown of creation'.

But does all this mean that there is no fundamental break in the process of evolution, no division of this world into two halves, as if the laws of nature ruled exclusively in the one, and the direct intervention of a divine creator in the other? Hence the question: 'What would be a divine incarnation in such a cosmic, biological, anthropological evolution, an absolutely particular event in such a universal happening? Or can we perhaps think of an incarnation which does not presuppose the naive religious assertion of a miraculous divine "intervention", "coming-in-between". An incarnation which does not interrupt the causal sequence, which does not represent any direct "supernatural" descent into the otherwise undisturbed process of nature?' But here a first almost insurmountable difficulty already emerges in the Apostles' Creed.

1. Do we believe in a virgin birth?

With this statement of faith, too, many people do not so much have definitions of belief as pictures of belief in mind: pictures of the incarnation, of the annunciation to Mary, and Jesus' birth. Who does not know the picture of the annunciation to Mary which has become a classic, painted by a Dominican monk between 1436 and 1445 – about half a century before Michelangelo's frescoes – , large but coherently structured, in what was then the new monastery of San Marco in Florence, on the wall of a monastic cell? The monk was, of course, Fra Giovanni da Fiesole, who after his death was called Fra Angelico.

'Beato Angelico': the only artist whom the church has ever called 'beatus', 'blessed'. 'Beatus', not of course because at the transition from the beautiful, soft, courtly, refined style of waning international Gothic to the early Italian Renaissance he replaced the golden background with landscape and the flatness with scientifically correct perspectives and vivid figure painting, or because decorative details were less important to him than classic simplicity. 'Blessed', rather, because in the midst of the lively Florence of Cosimo di Medici he painted for the meditation of the monks in unaffected, tranquil contemplativeness.

Against a pillared hall in perfect perspective, like that of the courtyard of San Marco, and in a quite distinctive harmony of bright colours, on the wall of this cell we can see two attractive figures turned to each other in conversation: on the left in delicate rose with splendid coloured wings is the angel, and on the right, sitting on a footstool in a pale red dress and blue cloak, is the Virgin Mary – in humble terror at the angel's greeting and what it means. 'You have found grace with God. Behold, you will be with child and bear a son and you will give him the name Jesus' (Luke 1.30f.). This art used to be called 'vezzoso', attractive, pleasant, and '*ornato*', tasteful, painted with great '*facilità*', ease, effortlessness. At any rate it is a combination of mediaeval-naive belief and admirably simple early-Renaissance scenery. A *hortus conclusus*, a blossoming garden shut off by a fence from the tall trees in the background: evidently a symbol for the conception of Jesus by Mary, the virgin, without male procreation. A picture between day and dream.

'But,' I hear contemporaries saying, 'surely that is more dream than day! More image than sense! More *mythos* than *logos*! Surely you don't want us as it were to hold our breath, like nature in Fra Angelico's picture, so as not to disturb the hallowed moment? Surely you don't want to entice us in the twentieth century with this devotional picture from the fifteenth century, exceptionally beautiful though it may be, to confess "Jesus Christ . . . conceived by the Holy Spirit (*conceptus de Spiritu Sancto*) born of the Virgin Mary (*natus ex Maria Virgine*)"?'

But perhaps here as a theologian I can summon the aid of psychology, and above all depth psychology, in the face of this difficult problem? But should I, may I?

2. Belief in Christ in the age of psychotherapy

As is well known, Freud had a great rival in psychotherapy, who was better able to cope with religion than he was, since as a result of materialist science Freud had become an atheist: the Swiss Carl Gustav Jung, founder of 'complex psychology'. In many of his writings Jung also accepted the Christian symbols of faith in particular, using them to investigate the psychological depth-structures which had become manifest here. These included the 'symbol' of the virgin birth. For Jung the 'divine child', born of the virgin, is a primal image, one of those notions which have become established in the unconscious, which have come down to us genetically from primal times and are common to all human beings, one of the representations originally of instinctive, psychologically necessary reactions to particular situations – comparable to other primal images: the mother, the radiant hero, the evil spirit, the dragon, the snake. In Jung's terminology the image of the divine, saving, redeeming child is an archetype, a primal model of the soul. It is expressed in different images and experiences, developments and views, particularly in the context of strong experiences in human life like birth, puberty, love, danger, deliverance and death.

Jung did not invent the famous term 'archetype'. It was originally a theological concept and came from the Gnostic arcane doctrine of the *Corpus Hermeticum*, dating from late antiquity. Jung took it over above all from the writings of Dionysius the Areopagite, the alleged disciple of Paul (he mediated Eastern mysticism to the West in the fifth and sixth centuries), and from the work of Augustine, who had rooted Plato's eternal ideas as *ideae principales* in the divine intellect. But whereas the ideal primal images of Plato and Augustine are of the supreme perfection of light, the archetypes of Jung, who drew his insights from his therapeutic practice and from his preoccupation with the religious traditions of ancient peoples, had a bipolar, ambivalent structure, and show both a light and a dark side.

Now what is the meaning of the archetype of the 'divine child, born of a virgin', which has found the most varied expression at all times and in all peoples, in fairy tale and myth, in art and in religion? According to Jung the divine child is for our dreams and myths the great symbol of the 'unbegotten', not made, in our individual or indeed collective psyche. This 'virgin' figure is opposed to the figure of the male, i.e. reason, understanding. The language of the unconscious is in fact a language of images determined by feelings. Myths, sagas, fairy tales are thus something like objectified dreams. So, too, with the divine child. It is an archetype, and like all archetypes an inexhaustible source of age-old knowledge about the deepest connections between human beings, the world and God.

No wonder that in this perspective the symbol of the divine child born of the virgin also already appears in the Bible. Strikingly, however, not yet in the Hebrew Bible, for in the famous Emmanuel prophecy of the book of Isaiah (7.14) there is mention only of a young woman (Hebrew *alma*) who will bear a son to whom she gives the name 'Immanuel' = God with us. In the Greek translation of the Hebrew Bible, however, *alma* was (wrongly) translated *parthenos*, 'virgin', and so this passage also found its way into the New Testament as Old Testament 'proof' of the virginity of the mother of the Messiah. Thus the idea of the divine child and the virgin stands in the miraculous entrance hall to the great Gospels of Matthew and Luke, both of whom alone in the New Testament offer an account of Jesus' infancy with a genealogy and naming of parents, with begetting by the Spirit and virgin birth.

So it can hardly be surprising that not a few theologians in Europe and America, both male and female, today feel stimulated to bring to consciousness the unsuspected treasure of human depth experience which also appears specifically in the biblical writings. And as one who forty years ago as a student of philosophy made an intensive study of his fellow-countryman C.G. Jung, I can now rejoice and defend such action against the inquisitors in Rome and Germany who feel such exegesis in the service of psychotherapy to be subversive and a danger to faith, and learn nothing from their countless official errors over matters of faith and morals. There are many levels of meaning in the Bible, and so too there must be many approaches to the Bible; no method is the only one with the seal of divine approval. And given such pluralism of method, why should not the depth-psychological method of biblical interpretation also be allowed?

So one can only assent to what the theologian and psychotherapist Eugen Drewermann has attempted – in the wake of some others: to interpret the Bible and thus also the infancy story of Jesus along the lines of C.G.Jung, a story which has been over-dogmatized by the church tradition and completely demythologized by historical-critical exegesis. One can only be glad if Drewermann succeeds in making the biblical narrative more understandable to some contemporaries with the help of depth psychology – and against the background of material from the comparative history of religion which has long since been worked over by historical criticism. Drewermann wants to make these images – and it is primarily a matter of images and not words – speak again. People in our day are to be helped in the encounter with these images to free themselves from the ghetto of existential anxiety and find their own identity. The binding element, the uniting factor between the cultures and religions of all times and zones, lies in the archetypes and the feelings, whereas language, reason, the moral tables of categories and values, time-conditioned as they are, prove to be divisive. It is the task of biblical

37

exegesis with the help of depth psychology to interpret the archetypal narratives, for which detached historical-critical research has no sense, with every technique and rule available, in such a way that human beings may be helped to trust and to self-discovery.

And what does that mean for the stories about Jesus' infancy? Here, too, exegesis inspired by depth psychology seeks to investigate biblical symbols like virgin birth in their abiding supra-temporal truth for the understanding of faith. According to Drewermann, as the New Testament depicts the birth and childhood of the redeemer, it paints 'in all the archetypal sequences of action, the stages which must necessarily be undergone in the life of all human beings if they are to regain a true life for themselves in the light of God': 'The miracle of the virgin birth is grounded *in the life of human beings themselves* (I emphasize the decisive words) if only they hearken to their own being; *in their own souls lies* the initially despised figure of the "mother", regarded as a whore, who at the same time in the light of the angelic message ultimately shows herself to be Madonna; *in themselves* there is Joseph, ready-to-hear, dreaming, angel-understanding, bold, and the magi who followed a star from the land of the dawn; but there is also *in them* a Herod who himself acts against the express word of God and in the terror of his anxiety spreads only murder and death; *in themselves* there is the proud city of Jerusalem and insignificant Bethlehem, where alone according to ancient prophecies the salvation of the world can be born; there are *in every human soul* places of refuge and places of determination – and all this together takes shape in the example of the history of Jesus as the model narrative of all human beings on the way *to their incarnation* and humanity.'[12] All this means that 'All individuals bear before God the call to become in themselves an "implanted" (Messiah) of God, a "man from Nazareth" (Matt.2.23). Indeed it is always also through the image of the dream and the voice of the unconscious reason of our soul that we hear God's voice.'[13]

There is no doubt that the historical-critical method – which today in any case is a complex combination of a variety of methods from linguistics to sociology – needs to be supplemented by depth psychology. And yet questions must be asked here. Is the Bible primarily myth and not history? Doesn't the Hebrew Bible already represent the unique documentation in the history of religion of a radical criticism of myth in the name of the one God? Don't myths – in so far as they appear in the Bible at all – at the very most have history as a constituent element, so that here, in contrast to some other religions, it is not simply a matter of the appearance of the eternal in time? And should myth, saga, fairy tale in principle have precedence over the Logos, the word? Is there to be remythologizing instead of demythologizing? Has the dream, important as it is, to be set over the word and as it were be promoted to a methodological key for the whole interpretation of the Bible?

At any rate, questions arise in the face of a monopoly of interpretation by depth psychology: certainly these biblical stories of Jesus' infancy are not about historical (or imaginary) biographical facts, and they may also be read as symbolic descriptions of nature which today tell us something about our own psychological possibilities, in so far as we open ourselves to the divine. It is understandable that a psychologist like Jung should only ask about psychological truth, but what about a critical theologian? 'If psychology speaks, for example, of the motif of the virgin birth,' says Jung, 'it is only concerned with the fact that there is such an idea, it is not concerned with the question whether such an idea is true or false in any other sense. The idea is psychologically true inasmuch as it exists.'[14] But may one separate psychological truth in this way from actual, historical truth? Mustn't we continually ask the authors of the texts what they themselves wanted to say? May the theologian then neglect the historical element of the Bible as irrelevant or even eliminate it, as though this were one of Grimm's fairy tales in which it is a matter of complete indifference whether or not Little Red Riding Hood ever lived? Erich Fromm rightly comments critically on Jung's view of religion: 'Even the practising psychiatrist could not work were he not concerned with the truth of an idea. Otherwise he would not be able to speak of a delusion or a paranoid system.'[15]

And as far as Drewermann is concerned, the key word 'truth' is missing from his two great volumes on *Depth Psychology and Exegesis*. The biblical infancy narratives certainly do not seek to explain the mystery of Jesus but to transfigure it; they do not seek to prove but to indicate; do not seek to understand but to grasp. But are historical detachment and existential involvement necessarily exclusive? And more important: isn't it rather immodest to commandeer all these texts and persons for psychology if they can hardly express their primal meaning any longer? Mary, Joseph and the child, the Magi, Herod and the angels, the star, the city of Jerusalem, Egypt, Bethlehem and Nazareth, do they all, lock, stock and barrel, as Drewermann says, become 'the figures and zones of one soul, one soulscape'?[16]

No, here we must ask: is the dream really the father of all things? In these strongly legendary infancy narratives isn't there more than mere dreams? Are the images really more important than the words, the feelings more important than the actions? Isn't a message clearly being given which is considerably more than just a psychotherapeutic introduction to the finding of identity, more than a help to life which, if necessary, one can derive directly from Jung even without the Bible? In the Bible, aren't God's revelations as a whole bound more to historical events than to dreams? And are the stories about Jesus' infancy really only or even primarily about a 'soulscape', my soulscape, even my soulscape analysed by this therapist with the aid of the Jungian method? Do I really already have the 'divine child', the redeemer, within myself, so that I only need to become conscious of him in order myself to become a 'man from Nazareth'? I – the 'man from Nazareth', 'the Messiah'? No, in this way the unique and irreplaceable historical figure of Jesus of Nazareth seems to be absorbed all too much into the state of my soul! There, moreover, this Jesus can never do more than keep repeating the same psychotherapeutic truths, which are certainly all-important, but centre on liberation from anxiety and dependence, on trust and love, and thus on the self-becoming of human beings from within, in their different stages of life.

Some contemporaries, already impatient, won't want too much psychology and psychotherapy: 'How long are you yourself going to go on dodging the question of truth, the question whether Jesus was historically born of a virgin, whether the virgin birth really happened, as is preached from so many pulpits on the Feast of the Annunciation (25 March, nine months before the festival of Christ's birth) and even more at Christmas itself?' Granted, in view of the fact that biologists today radically rule out 'parthogenesis' (procreation by a duplication of the feminine hereditary substance), simply on the basis of the different formation of male and female genes not only in human beings but also in higher forms of life, one cannot simply settle this question in our scientific-industrial world, in which some technological 'miracles' far surpass the biblical miracles, with an appeal to a 'miracle' in the face of all the laws of nature. But what is the position of this 'miracle' in scripture?

3. Virgin birth – a biological fact?

Having attempted to take seriously three centuries of empirical scientific research in connection with the first article of faith about God the Father, I must now take no less seriously two centuries of historical-critical biblical research in connection with the article of faith in Jesus Christ, the Son. Granted, even if I wanted to, I couldn't dodge the historical problems which obviously arise here. For even the simple Bible reader – someone confronted not only with the biblical images (in the Middle Ages the *Biblia pauperum*, 'the Bible of the Poor'), but also with the biblical texts – can very easily establish that the infancy narratives are very different from the public life of Jesus. All too much happens in dreams, and angels constantly go to and fro. Is that meant to be historical? Furthermore, aren't there contradictions between the two infancy narratives which cannot be harmonized? Whereas Matthew seems to know nothing of Nazareth as the abode of the mother of Jesus, conversely Luke seems to know nothing of the public events (not mentioned in secular sources) of the visit of the Magi, the massacre of the innocents in Bethlehem and the flight to Egypt – mostly scenes which Fra Angelico also painted in San Marco. So the question becomes more pressing: are such stories at all historically credible?

Even Catholic exegetes now concede that – although the use of historical material cannot be excluded – the stories of Jesus' childhood are largely historically uncertain, highly legendary narratives with a stamp of their own, which in the last resort have a theological motivation. But what is theology, what is the meaning of these stories? Certainly not just what according to the depth-psychological interpretation of the image of the divine child is the 'general permission', namely, in the end to be able to 'begin' with trust and to live inwardly without anxiety: self-discovery. Rather, the infancy narratives, if they are not historical accounts, are by no means unpolitical stories of confession and proclamation. They might come from the Jewish-Christian communities, have been worked over by Matthew and Luke, and then have been prefaced to their Gospels. They say that Jesus is the 'Messiah' of Israel. He is not just a 'child'; he is the Christ of his people. Indeed, he is the awaited Son of David; he is the new Moses. So Matthew and Luke take the trouble on the one hand to trace back the genealogy of Jesus to David, and on the other to give clear hints of the story of Moses. Just as Moses as a child was rescued from Pharaoh, so too Jesus was rescued – by his flight with his parents. There are also models and parallels in the Hebrew Bible for the infancy narratives in Matthew and Luke. So the stories of the Old and New Testaments are as it were coupled. And Egyptian literature also knows ideas of this kind.

'But,' a contemporary interrupts at this point, 'surely it's beyond dispute that the virgin birth is a myth which was widespread in antiquity, from Egypt to India?' Certainly that is the case, and I personally agree with the Tübingen Egyptologist Emma Brunner-Traut, who writes in her fine article on 'Pharaoh and Jesus as Sons of God': 'There is evidence in Egypt for virtually all the episodes of the miracle of Christmas, just as individual features of the later life and activity of the son of Mary have their counterparts . . . The birth ritual of the divine child which was shaped into the (Egyptian) royal dogma . . . was also incorporated into the Osiris mysteries in the Ptolemaic Hellenistic period, and from there it has exercised its influence on the whole of the Eastern Mediterranean; the influence of the Hellenistic-Egyptian mysteries on the formation of the Jewish-Christian "legends" can hardly be rated too highly.'[17]

Indeed, as divine king the Pharaoh of Egypt is conceived miraculously: from the Spirit God Amon-Re in the form of the ruling king and the virgin queen. But also in Greek-Hellenistic mythology, gods enter into 'sacred marriages' with the daughters of men, from whom sons of God like Perseus and Heracles or even historical figures like Homer, Plato, Alexander and Augustus can emerge. There is no mistaking the fact that in itself the virgin birth is not something exclusively Christian! Moreover, contemporary exegesis believes that the theme of the virgin birth is used as an 'aetiological' legend or saga which is meant to provide a 'reason' (Greek *aitia*) in retrospect for the divine Sonship.

Nevertheless, the differences between the two New Testament narratives and the ancient myths are significant (and Fra Angelico saw this intuitively):

– The annunciation and reception of the event of conception by Mary takes place in the word, without any intercourse between God and human beings, in a completely unerotic, spiritualized context. Mary does not appear as a heavenly being who bestows grace, but as a human being who is given grace, who bears witness not only to Jesus' true humanity but also to Jesus' origin in God. So Mary is significant for Christian piety as the mother of Jesus, as the example and model for Christian faith, and as the prophetic witness to the mighty acts of God ('Magnificat').

– The Holy Spirit is not understood as begetting partner or father, but as the active power of the conception of Jesus. Crude personifications of the Holy Spirit, the power and might of God, are ruled out, since in the biblical scenes the Holy Spirit cannot be seen even in the form of a dove. In contrast to the original formulation of, say, the Roman Creed – 'born of the Holy Spirit and the Virgin Mary' – from the fourth century there is a distinction: 'conceived by the Holy Spirit' (*conceptus de . . .*) and 'born of Mary' (*natus ex . . .*).

So is the virgin birth already an expression of tendencies in Christianity which are hostile to the body, sex and marriage? Be this as it may, in the New Testament there is not yet that high stylization of the virginity of Mary so that it becomes the great ideal, which for many of our contemporaries has become symptomatic of the 'sexual hang-ups' of the church . . . At the same time, it is impossible to refrain here from saying something about the virgin birth which is fundamental for both therapists and theologians: outside the two Gospels which I have mentioned, the virgin birth of Jesus is simply not known anywhere else in the New Testament. For this reason alone, it cannot be regarded as original or central to the Christian message. In the letters of Paul, the earliest documents of the New Testament, there is no more than a terse mention, without any names, of the birth of Jesus 'from a woman' (Gal.4.4) but not 'from a virgin' – in order to stress Jesus' humanity.

The earliest Gospel, that of Mark, has no birth narratives at all, and without any dreams begins immediately with John the Baptist and Jesus' public life and teaching, about which unfortunately there is nothing in the Apostles' Creed. Should not 'Mariologists' take the exegetical evidence more seriously? In Mark, we hear only once about Mary – apart from the mention of her name along with the names of Jesus' four brothers and sisters (Mark 6.3): that is when Jesus' mother and brothers think him crazy and want to bring him home by force (Mark 3.21, 31-35). According to all three Synoptic Gospels Mary does not appear either under the cross or in the Easter stories. Only the late Gospel of John, written around 100, reports an evidently symbolic scene under the cross (John 19.25-27), but like all the other New Testament witnesses, it too knows nothing of a virgin birth.

This leads to the momentous conclusion that evidently the virgin birth does not belong at the centre of the gospel. It is not only not exclusively Christian, but is not even centrally Christian. In other words, like Mark, Paul or John, one could confess Jesus as the Messiah, Christ or Son of God even if one knew nothing of the virgin birth. And what does that mean for today? For our contemporaries it means that belief in Christ in no way stands or falls with the confession of the virgin birth.

This may have prepared us to give a clear answer to the question of the historical reality and theological meaning of the virgin birth: the narrative of the virgin birth is not a report of a biological fact but the interpretation of reality by means of a primal symbol. It is a very striking symbol: with Jesus God makes a truly new beginning – in the history of the world and not just in the life of my soul. The origin and significance of Jesus' person and fate are not explained only in terms of the immanent course of history, but for believers are ultimately to be understood in terms of the action of God through it and in it. That is the christological and theological meaning of this story of the virgin birth. But then as now, this meaning can also be proclaimed in a different way – for example by tracing Jesus' genealogy back to God or interpreting

Jesus as a 'second Adam' (as Paul did) or as the 'Word made flesh' (as John did).

But I hear the objection: 'Doesn't such historical criticism destroy the message of Christmas and in this way further intensify the superficial secularization and active commercialization of this festival?' That is a legitimate question. But we need to reflect that not only the historical criticism and the secularization and commercialization, but also the transformation of Christmas into an innocuous idyll and its psychological privatization, can empty the Christmas message and the Christmas festival of meaning. It is not just the rationalistic Enlightenment and a remythologizing romanticism – whether psychological or Mariological – which can dissolve the creed. What is usually overlooked in psychotherapeutic and dogmatic interpretation must now be clearly brought out:

4. The political dimension of Christmas

We saw that even if the birth narratives are not the accounts of a historian, they are true in their way and announce a truth which is more than the truth of historical facts. This can be done more pictorially and impressively in the form of a single legendary story of the child in a manger in Bethlehem than by a birth certificate which provides a date and a location, however unobjectionable that may be. We must simply reflect again on the original biblical texts of Jesus' birth in a historical context to understand why the creed also talks of Jesus Christ 'our Lord': Dominus noster.

Here against the background of the religious and political rule of the time and those exercising it we can see something like the nucleus of a liberation theology which forms the necessary political counterbalance to contemporary psycho-theology. One has only to read this Christmas story carefully and note:
– Nowhere is there talk of a 'silent night' and a 'gentle infant, so tender and bright': manger, swaddling clothes, are concrete signs of a world of lowliness and poverty.
– The saviour of those in need, born in a manger, clearly reveals an option for those without name and power (the 'shepherds') over against the authorities who are mentioned by name (the emperor Augustus, the imperial governor Quirinius).

– The Magnificat of Mary, 'the handmaid of the Lord' full of grace, which speaks of the humiliation of the mighty and the exaltation of the lowly, of the filling of the hungry and the sending away empty of the rich, militantly proclaims a reversal of values and status.

– The blessed night of the newborn child cannot be detached from its influence and its destiny three decades later: the child in a manger as it were already bears the sign of the cross on his forehead.

– The community's complete confession of faith is already expressed in the scenes of the Annunciation (to Mary and the shepherds) which in fact now make up the heart of the Christmas story, as later in the trial before the Jewish tribunal, by a number of titles set side by side: Son of God, Saviour, Messiah, King, indeed Lord. This is done in such a way as to give lordship to this child rather than to the emperor Augustus.

– And finally, instead of the deceptive Pax Romana, bought with raised taxes, an escalation in armaments, pressure on the minorities and the pessimism of prosperity, with 'great joy' the true Pax Christi is announced: it has its foundation in a new order of interpersonal relationships under the sign of God's loving kindness and peace among human beings.

– So the true peace is contrasted with the political saviour and the political theology of the Roman empire, which provided ideological support for the imperial peace policy. This cannot be expected where divine honour is offered to a human being, an autocrat or a theocrat, but only where glory is given to God 'in the highest' and his good pleasure rests on men and women. Now therapeutically peace in the soul *and* politically the end of wars, liberation from anxiety *and* a life worth living, universal happiness, in short universal well-being, the 'salvation' of human beings and the world, is no longer expected from the overwhelmingly powerful Roman emperor but from this helpless, powerless child.

Contemporaries can also understand that: the Christmas story, rightly understood, is anything but a harmlessly edifying or psychologically refined story of the dear child Jesus. All these biblical narratives are stories about Christ with a high degree of theological reflection, at the service of a proclamation with a very specific aim, which seeks to make clear in a way which is artistic, vivid and radically critical of society the significance of Jesus as the Messiah for the salvation of all the peoples of the earth. So these infancy narratives are not, say, the first phase of a biography of Jesus or an intimate family story, nor are they psychotherapeutic guidance which is not significantly different from an Egyptian myth. Rather, they are a powerful overture to the great Gospels of Matthew and Luke which (like so many good overtures) conveys in a nutshell the message which is later to be developed in narrative. They are a way into the gospel: in Jesus, the elect of God, the promises to the 'fathers' of the first covenant are fulfilled.

Thus it is clear that the events surrounding the birth of Jesus do not form the centre of the gospel. The centre is Jesus Christ himself, Jesus in his quite personal words, action and suffering. The centre is Jesus as alive, a person living and ruling in the Spirit even after his death. With his message, his conduct, his fate, he offers the supremely concrete criterion by which human beings can take their bearings. And this Jesus did not work through dreams and in dreams, but in the clear light of history. And although he himself did not write a word, although we have only texts which proclaim him and thus always only indirect historical accounts, it is certain beyond dispute that Jesus of Nazareth is a figure of history, and as such is distinct not only from all figures of myth, saga, fairy-tale and legend, but also from other important figures of the history of religion, not least living Indian religion, which is so rich in myths – and some of our contemporaries are even more interested in this than in Egyptian religion. That is important as we now turn to the question of divine Sonship, the question how this Jesus can be understood as God's revelation. Here a brief comparison between Jesus Christ and the divine Krishna may be illuminating.

5. Belief in Christ or Krishna – is it the same thing?

Krishna, the great hero of Indian mythology in the Indian national epic, the Mahabharata, is the best known of all deities. He is regarded as the incarnation (in Sanskrit the 'Avatar' = the 'descendant') of the one God (Vishnu). It was Krishna who brought the Bhagavad-Gita (the 'Song of the Exalted'), a didactic philosophical poem which is regarded as a kind of 'gospel' of

Hinduism. In the West, there is widespread ignorance of what many believing Hindus take for granted, namely that Krishna, too, is a historical person, to whose workplaces people make pilgrimages. If here I may introduce terms from classic christological dogma, he is an authentic man (*vere homo*), but at the same time he is the revelation of the one God (*vere Deus*).

That means that for Hindus, too, the one God has revealed himself at a particular place at a particular time. For Hindus, too, there is a decisive action of God within a cyclical history of the world which, as in the case of Krishna, has as it were end-time (eschatological) character for this world age. So this 'Avatara', this 'descent' of God in Krishna, who has brought the good news of the Bhagavad-Gita, is fundamental revelation for Hinduism. Against this background we can understand the saying that is widespread among tolerant Hindus: 'You believe in Christa, we in Krishna – it's the same thing!' Thus a parallel between the Christ child and the Krishna child, between belief in Christ and belief in Krishna, cannot be denied. But are they both really the same thing under different names? That is the question.

It is beyond dispute that Krishna, too, is a historical person, though he can be dated and located only very vaguely, in connection with the battle on the Kuru field, to post-Vedic times, and every possible kind of traditional material has attached itself to his figure. But even if the outlines were clearer and the state of historical research better, the differences between Krishna and Christ equally cannot be overlooked:

– First, Jesus Christ is not, like Krishna, a fusion of different mythical and historical figures: Krishna is already mentioned in an Upanishad (eighth century), but takes on increasing significance only many centuries later, through his identification with Krishna Vasudeva, the founder of the religion of the monotheistic Bhagavatas, who already in the second century taught loving surrender to God (*bhakti*) as the way of salvation.

– Secondly, Jesus Christ is not, like Krishna, one revelation or incarnation of God among many: Krishna is understood as a revelation of the God Vishnu, indeed as his eighth, which will be followed by a ninth (= Buddha) and a last (= Kalkin).

We cannot overlook the fact that in belief in Krishna we have an indication of that barely formed historical consciousness which

48

is characteristic of cyclical Indian thought. Because the figure of Krishna is fused from a number of traditions, there is no avoiding what the Christian community was able to prevent in the case of the person of Jesus, who can be dated and located clearly, by the canonization of the New Testament. A mass of highly questionable myths – at least seen in the light of the ethical level of the Bhagavad-Gita – could be connected with the figure of Krishna: one has only to compare some of the stories of Krishna's tricks and pranks, love affairs and adulteries, with the Gospels, which in their combination of history and kerygma, history and proclamation, are not only a distinctive literary genre but also documents of extraordinary moral earnestness.

However, that other great figure of Indian history, who in the fifth/fourth centuries set the 'wheel of doctrine' in motion there, Buddha Gautama, is quite comparable with the historical figure of Jesus of Nazareth. He is the great contrast figure among the founders of religion and – far more than Moses, Muhammad or Confucius – is the great alternative to Jesus of Nazareth, an alternative which is a continual challenge to our thought.

6. The challenge of the Buddha

Romano Guardini recognized this very early and made the point in this way: 'There is only one who could prompt the idea of putting him near to Jesus: Buddha. This man is a great mystery. He stands in a terrifying, almost superhuman freedom; at the same time he has a goodness, he is as powerful as a world force. Perhaps Buddha will be the last one with whom Christianity has to contend. No one has yet said what he means for Christianity. Perhaps Christ had not only a forerunner from the Old Testament, John, the last prophet, but also one from the heart of ancient culture, Socrates, and a third who spoke the last word of Eastern religious knowledge and overcoming, Buddha.'[18] So it is worth investigating the question: what do Christ and Buddha have in common and what distinguishes them?

Like 'the Christ', 'the anointed', so too 'the Buddha', 'the Enlightened' (literally 'the Awakened', 'who has achieved knowledge') is an honorific title. However, Buddha Gautama no more called himself God than did the Christ Jesus. Still, later generations saw Buddha not only as the wise man but as the redeemer, to whom people cried as a helper in time of need, and gave veneration (*puja*) – seeing him as superior to all gods – which was expressed through symbolic actions, for example offerings before the altar. That means that just as the Jesus of history is not simply identical with the ideas of Christ in later Christian theology, so too the Gautama of history is not simply identical with the images of Buddha in the later Buddhist schools.

In contrast to mythological Hindu popular religion and Krishna, probably its most famous figure, with Buddha, too, at the beginning we do not have myth, but history which leads to myth: the story of Siddhartha Gautama, the prince and later ascetic, who after long practice in profound contemplation became the 'Awakened' one, the Buddha, one who points the way from this life full of suffering to a state of ultimate rest beyond impermanence and suffering.

Certainly, Buddhist piety too decked this story at a very early stage with a series of miraculous events. The conception of the Buddha, like that of Christ, does not take place in the normal human way; rather, the heavenly seer and Bodhisattva 'as a young white elephant . . . entered the right side of his mother's body' and at birth 'emerged from his mother's right side. He was fully conscious and not sullied with the pollution of his mother's body.'[19] Numerous miracle stories are also told of Gautama, as of Jesus, and no serious historian doubts the fact that Jesus did charismatic healings. But there is no historical evidence in the case of either Gautama or Jesus for miracles in the strict modern sense of a 'supernatural' abolition of the laws of nature.

So if what is called Jesus' 'divine Sonship' were reduced to such extraordinary events at birth or miraculous events in his life and death, Jesus Christ would not be essentially different from Buddha or other non-Christian religious founders. 'But what,' the contemporary will ask, 'then really distinguishes Christ Jesus from the other normative figures in the history of religion, and from the Buddha in particular?' In order to approach this difficult question carefully, we must begin from certain external and indeed internal similarities between Gautama and Jesus, which are amazing.

Luton Central Library

Luton Central Library

www.lutonlibraries.co.uk

01582 547418

XXXXX5389

Item Title	Due Date
* CREDO. THE APOSTLES'	22/10/2011

* Indicates items borrowed today

For information call
01582 547418

7. What Jesus and Gautama have in common

In any case, some basic ethical instructions are the same in Buddhism as in the whole Judaeo-Christian-Islamic tradition: do not murder, do not steal, do not lie, do not commit adultery... These are ethical imperatives of humanity which could serve as irrevocable criteria for a common human ethic, a world ethic. Only the prohibition of intoxicants is something that Jesus does not mention, and that is no coincidence, since he is no ascetic and is said often to have gone to banquets, where of course wine was served.

But it is certain that in all his conduct Jesus shows more similarity with Gautama than, say, with Muhammad, the prophet, general and statesman, who enjoyed life to the end, or even with Confucius, the far-Eastern sage, orientated on an idealized old age and interested in the observance of the ancient rites, who advocated social order and harmony in family and state:

– Like Gautama, Jesus was an itinerant preacher – poor, homeless, with no claims, who had experienced a decisive turning-point in his life which had moved him to preaching.

– Like Gautama, in his preaching Jesus did not make use of a sacral language which had become incomprehensible (Sanskrit – Hebrew) but of the vernacular (central Indo-Aryan dialect – Aramaic vernacular). He did not write anything down or even arrange for a codification of his teaching.

– Like Gautama, Jesus appeals to human reason and capacity for knowledge, if not with reflective lectures and dialogues, then with generally understandable, memorable proverbs, short stories, similes taken from unadorned daily life and accessible to all, without resorting to formulae, dogmas and mysteries.

– As for Gautama, so too for Jesus, avarice, power and blindness represented the great temptation which – according to the temptation stories in the New Testament – stood in the way of his great task.

– Like Gautama, Jesus, too, not legitimated by any office, stood in opposition to religious tradition and its guardians, to the formalistic, ritualistic caste of priests and scribes who showed so little sensitivity to the suffering of the people.

– Like Gautama, Jesus, too, soon had very close friends around him: his circle of disciples and a wider following.

But there is a fundamental similarity not only in their conduct but also in their preaching.

– Like Gautama, Jesus appeared essentially as a teacher; the authority of both lay less in their scholastic training than in the extraordinary experience of an ultimate reality.

– Like Gautama, Jesus, too, had an urgent, joyful message to deliver (*dharma*, the 'gospel'), which required people to change their minds ('getting into the stream', *metanoia*) and to trust (*shraddha*, 'faith'): not orthodoxy but orthopraxy.

– Like Gautama, Jesus did not seek to give an explanation of the world: he did not engage in any profound philosophical speculation or learned legal casuistry; his teachings are no secret revelations about the nature of the kingdom of God; they are not even focussed on a particular order of worldly law and life.

– Like Gautama, Jesus, too, begins from the provisionality and transitoriness of the world, the impermanence of all things and the unredeemed nature of human beings: their blindness, folly, entanglement in the world and their lack of love towards their fellow human beings.

– Like Gautama, Jesus shows a way of redemption from selfishness, slavery to the world and blindness: a liberation which is not achieved by theoretical speculation but by a religious experience and an inner transformation; a quite practical way to salvation.

– As with Gautama, so too with Jesus, no particular presuppositions of an intellectual, moral or ideological kind are made on the way to this salvation: human beings are to hear, understand and draw their own conclusions. No one is examined on true faith, or on orthodox confessions.

– Like the way of Gautama, so too the way of Jesus is a middle way between the extremes of sensual delight and self-mortification, between permissive hedonism and rigorous asceticism, a way which makes possible a new unselfish concern for fellow human beings; not only do the general moral commandments of Buddha and Jesus largely coincide, but also, in principle, the 'dispositional ethic' and the basic demands of goodness and shared joy, of loving compassion (Buddha) and compassionate love (Jesus).

But great though the similarity may be in the whole conduct and basic features of the preaching and attitude of these two figures, so too is the dissimilarity in detail, in concrete formation and in practical realization.

8. *Where Jesus and Gautama differ*

According to the New Testament witnesses, Jesus did not come from a family of rich, aristocratic landowners; he did not grow up, as according to tradition Gautama acknowledged himself to have done, spoilt, very spoilt, with feasts and all kinds of luxuries. No, Jesus evidently came from a family of manual workers who could hardly have allowed themselves those excesses which drove so many rich sons like Gautama to tire of life and then flee their parental home.

Unlike Gautama, Jesus did not primarily address himself to contemporaries sated with civilization who in disgust at life wanted to rise above a society of excesses. Supported by no party or human authority, without laying claim to any honorific titles or making his own role or dignity the theme of his message, he turned to the weary and heavy-laden, the poor, whom he did not bless because poverty was an admirable ideal but because these had still retained an openness to that other reality with which he was concerned.

Jesus was not a solitary among solitaries (= *monachus*, monk), struggling for the one thing. He was the master in an alternative community of disciples, men and women, for whom he did not prescribe any orders, any rules, oaths, ascetic commandments or even any special clothes and traditions.

For Jesus the world was not a vanity, which it was important to abandon and which could be seen through in the act of contemplation: far less is it simply to be identified with the Absolute. Rather, it is the good creation, though constantly spoiled by human beings.

The turning point in Jesus' life does not involve giving up a wrong way and seeking his own redemption; he never refers to a special experience of enlightenment or conversion. For him the turning point is an emergence into public view from concealment: not a move inwards, but a move towards the world out of a remarkable immediacy to the one God of Israel whom – in scandalous familiarity – he addressed as 'Abba', 'dear Father', a term which at the same time expresses both distance and nearness, power and security. So here the aim is not an ascent from a cycle of births through one's own efforts, but entry into the consummation, the ultimate kingdom of God.

We can make the difference between Gautama and Jesus clearest if we refer back to the distinction between mystical and prophetic religion as it was developed by Friedrich Heiler and others and has more recently been applied to the Buddha Gautama and Christ Jesus by Gustav Mensching. Seen in this perspective, both the Buddha and the Christ each have their own greatness:

– The Buddha Gautama is an enlightened pioneer with a mystical spirit, resting harmoniously in himself:

– Sent by no one, for redemption from suffering in Nirvana he calls on people to turn away inwards from the world, to methodical meditations in stages of contemplation and thus finally to enlightenment. So in equanimity, without any personal involvement, he offers sympathy, gentleness and friendliness to any creature with feeling – man and beast: a universal compassion and peaceful benevolence.

– But the Christ Jesus is a passionately inspired ambassador and pioneer with a prophetic spirit and, for many people even during his lifetime, the Anointed ('Messiah', 'Christ').

– For redemption from guilt and all evil, in the kingdom of God, he calls on people to repent: instead of abandoning the will he appeals specifically to the human will, which he requires to be guided by the will of God that is wholly aimed at the all-embracing well-being, salvation, of human beings. So he is personally involved in proclaiming love, which includes all those who suffer, the oppressed, the sick, those who have incurred guilt and also those who are opponents and enemies: a universal love and active beneficence.

So – if we keep to the historical perspective – in the last resort, what is the fundamental difference between Jesus and Gautama?

9. The Illuminated and the Crucified

We probably see the decisive difference only when we venture to put side by side the figure of the smiling Buddha, sitting on a lotus blossom, and that of the suffering Jesus, nailed to the cross. Only from this historical perspective can we rightly understand the very much more comprehensive significance of the Buddha for Buddhists and the Christ for Christians.

Through his enlightenment the Buddha Gautama entered Nirvana – already accessible in this life – and after that lived for decades as the Enlightened One until finally, through death from a trivial cause, he entered into the final Nirvana, Parinirvana. Although not without pain and suffering, he lived at least cheerfully, harmoniously and successfully, and finally became highly respected among the powerful; he disseminated his teaching, and the number of his disciples became countless. He died at the ripe old age of eighty from food posioning, but even so, peacefully, surrounded by his disciples. All over the world even today the statues of this Buddha still attest his relaxation, enlightenment, his peace, his deep harmony, indeed his cheerfulness.

The man from Nazareth is quite different. His public life did not last for decades, but at most three years, and possibly only a few dramatic months, before it was brought to a violent end in Jerusalem. An extremely tense history from beginning to end, shaped by a fatal conflict with the religious and political establishment, the hierarchy, his whole story is ultimately a history of suffering with arrest, flogging and finally execution in a cruel, shameful form. This life has nothing enlightened and perfect about it. It remains a fragment, a torso. A fiasco? At any rate, there is no trace of success during Jesus' lifetime; according to the reports that we have, this man died as one who was despised, outlawed and accursed. A solitary end in the utmost pain: avoided by his mother and his family, abandoned by his disciples and followers, evidently forgotten by his God. The last we hear of him is his cry on the cross. From then till now – and this is almost intolerable for both Buddhists and even Christians whose senses have not been dulled – he is the image of the sufferer *par excellence*. However, this is a suffering which the first Christian communities already did not understand as the sheer desperation of a failed man but as an act of the utmost surrender, ultimate love for God and human beings.

Truly, he was a sufferer who did not exude pity but himself demanded pity; who did not rest in himself but surrendered himself utterly. It is thus, as the one who suffers in dedication and love, that in Christian understanding this Jesus differs from the Buddha, the benevolent, the compassionate one. In this way he also differs unmistakably from all the many gods and deified founders of religions, and also differs from all religious geniuses and gurus, heroes and emperors of world history: as the sufferer, as the one who was executed, as the crucified one.

But regardless of his relationship to the Buddha, looking at Jesus any contemporary will feel driven to ask: 'How then does it happen that despite this shameful death there was a Jesus movement, indeed belief in Jesus, so that the Creed can say quite naturally: "I believe in Jesus Christ, the 'only' Son of God, this one and no other?" What a contrast: the crucified one – God's Son!' But:

10. What does it mean to say that God has a Son?

If we want to understand why Jesus' disciples came to proclaim Jesus God's Son, we should not begin from his birth but from his death. The dying cry of Jesus, 'My God, my God, why have you forsaken me?' (Mark 15.34), is already made positive in the Gospel of Luke with a quotation from the Psalms: 'Father, into your hands I commend my Spirit' (Ps.31.6; Luke 23.46), and finally in the Gospel of John with the words 'It is fulfilled' (19.30). Indeed, from the beginning this was the steadfast conviction of the first Christian community, which like the apostle Paul appealed to experiences: this crucified one has not fallen into nothingness, but from provisional, transitory, impermanent reality has entered into the true, eternal life of God. He is alive – however that is to be explained. And this, too, cannot mean any 'super-natural' intervention of a *deus ex machina*, as we shall see, but, as is indicated in Luke by 'into your hands' or in the Gospel of John with the 'lifting up', the 'natural' dying into and being taken up from death into the real, true reality: a final state which at all events is without any suffering.

Following the Apostles' Creed, I shall discuss the cross and resurrection separately, and then I shall also have to bring in the Jewish context of the story of Jesus more markedly. At this point my prime concern is to explain the title 'Son of God', and for that, in the light of present-day New Testament exegesis, the fundamental point is that Jesus never called himself God. On the contrary: 'Why do you call me good? No one is good save God alone' (Mark 10.18). Only after his death, when on the basis of particular Easter experiences, visions and auditions, people felt able to believe that he had not remained in suffering and death, but had been taken up into God's eternal life, had been 'exalted' by God to God, did the believing community begin to use the title 'Son' or 'Son of God' for Jesus.

Why? This might also have been quite possible for some Jews of the time (and here we come full circle and return to our starting point in the Gospels):

– First, we should remember the inner experience of God, bond with God and immediacy to God in which Jesus of Nazareth lived, preached and acted: how he taught that God should be regarded as the Father of all human beings ('Our Father') and himself called him Father ('Abba, dear Father'). So for Jews who were Jesus' disciples there was a pertinent reason and an inner logic why the followers who believed in him should have given the explicit title 'Son' to the one who had called God 'Father'. Not like the king of Israel in former times, since for a long time there had been no such king; but he, the Messiah who had been expected and had come, was now in a unique way God's Son.

– Secondly, people began to sing the hymns of the Psalter, understood in a messianic way, and especially the enthronement psalms, in honour of the one who had been raised from the dead. Jews at that time could easily understand the exaltation to God in analogy to the enthronement of the Israelite king. Just as the latter – probably on the basis of the royal ideology of the ancient Near East – was appointed 'Son of God' at the moment of his accession, so now the crucified one was was appointed 'Son' through his resurrection and exaltation.

It may have been Psalm 110 in particular, the psalm in which King David celebrated his future 'Son', who was at the same time his 'Lord', that was constantly sung and quoted: 'The Lord said to my Lord: Sit at my right hand!' (v.1). For as Martin Hengel has pointed out,[20] to Jesus' Jewish followers this verse was the answer to the burning question of the 'place' and function of the Risen One. Where is the Risen One now? The answer could be: with the Father, 'at the Father's right hand', not in a communion of being but in a throne-communion with the Father, so that kingdom of God and messianic kingdom in fact become identical: 'The appointment of the crucified Messiah Jesus as the "Son" with the Father "through the resurrection from the dead" is thus probably part of the oldest message, common to all preachers, with which the "messianic heralds" summoned their own people to conversion and to belief in the "Messiah of Israel" who had been crucified and raised by God and exalted to his right hand.'[21]

And indeed, in Psalm 2.7 – an enthronement ritual – the Messiah king is even addressed explicitly as 'son': 'You are my son; today I have begotten you.' It should be noted that here 'begetting' is a synonym for enthronement, exaltation. There is no trace either in the Hebrew Bible or in the New Testament of a physical-sexual procreation as in the case of the Egyptian god-king and the Hellenistic sons of God, or even of a metaphysical procreation in the sense of the later Hellenistic ontological doctrine of the Trinity.

So one of the oldest confessions of faith (which is probably already pre-Pauline) in the introduction to the letter to Romans can say that Jesus Christ was 'appointed Son of God in power from the resurrection of the dead' (Rom.1.4). Consequently, this enthronement Psalm 2 can be taken up in the Acts of the Apostles and now applied to Jesus: 'He (God) said to me (according to Ps.2.7, to the king, the anointed, but according to Acts 13.33 to Jesus): "You are my Son, today I have begotten you."' And why can all this happen? Because here, in the New Testament, the thought is still firmly Jewish: 'begotten' as king, 'begotten' as anointed (= Messiah, Christ) simply means appointed as representative and son. And in Acts the 'today' (in the Psalms the day of enthronement) clearly does not mean Christmas, but Easter; in other words, not the feast of the descent, the becoming-man, the 'incarnation', but the day of resurrection, the exaltation of Jesus to God, Easter, the chief feast of Christianity.

So what is the original Jewish and thus also New Testament

meaning of divine Sonship? Regardless of what is defined later by the Hellenistic councils with Hellenistic concepts here, the New Testament beyond question does not mean to speak of a descent but of the appointment to a position of justice and power in the Hebrew-Old Testament sense. This is not a physical divine Sonship, as is still often assumed in the Hellenistic myths and by Jews and Muslims, and rightly rejected, but an election and empowerment of Jesus, very much along the lines of the Hebrew Bible, where sometimes the people of Israel can also be collectively called 'Son of God'. There were hardly any basic objections to such an understanding of divine Sonship in the light of the Jewish belief in one God; otherwise the original Jewish community would certainly not have claimed it. If the divine Sonship were again claimed today as it was originally understood, it would seem that there would be few basic objections to it even today from Jewish and Islamic monotheism.

However, some contemporaries will not be convinced. 'Isn't the idea of an incarnation certainly un-Jewish, not to say nonsensical?'

11. The meaning of incarnation

There is no doubt about it: in time a christology of incarnation coming from above took its place alongside the original exaltation christology, conceived of as coming from below. Paul still speaks of a *'sending'* of the *Son* of God, but John already speaks of a *'becoming flesh'* of the *Word* of God – though neither speaks of the sending, becoming flesh, of God the Father himself, but of the sending of his Son, of his Word becoming flesh. How are we to understand that? Does this break down all the bridges with Judaism, as some people think?

In his great study of pre-existence christology, *Born Before All Time?*, my Tübingen colleague Karl-Josef Kuschel has been able to show convincingly that the Pauline statements about the sending of the Son of God do not presuppose any pre-existence of Christ as a heavenly being, understood in mythological terms, but must similarly be seen against a Jewish background, namely in the context of the prophetic tradition. As he points out: 'The metaphor of "sending" (borrowed from the prophetic tradition) expresses the conviction that the person and work of Jesus do not originate within history but are completely the result of God's initiative.'[22] 'Paul's confessions are about the origin, derivation and presence of Christ, from God and in God, but not about a temporally isolated "existence" before the creation of the world . . . For Paul, Christ is the crucified wisdom of God in person, not the personified pre-existent wisdom.'[23]

The same is to be said of the Gospel of John. In this late, fourth Gospel, too, God and his emissary are clearly distinguished: 'This is eternal life, that they should know you, the only true God, and Jesus Christ, whom you have sent' (John 17.3). Or, 'I am going to my Father and your Father, to my God and your God' (John 20.17). No, this Gospel too does not develop any speculative metaphysical christology – torn from its Jewish roots – but presents a christology which is still completely bound up with the world of Jewish Christianity, which is concerned with mission and revelation, yet in which the statement of pre-existence (understood in an unmythological sense) takes on heightened significance. However, such sayings about pre-existence do not have any speculative value, any independent theological significance, but have a narrowly limited 'function'; they are at the service of God's revelation and redemption through the Son who has been sent: 'John does not investigate the metaphysical nature and being of the pre-existent Christ: he is not concerned to know that before the incarnation there were two pre-existent divine persons bound together in the one divine nature.'[24] So what was John's positive concern? 'What stands in the foreground is the statement of the confession that the man Jesus of Nazareth is the Logos of God in person. And he is the Logos as a mortal man. However, he is the Logos only for those who are prepared to believe trusting God's word in his word, God's actions in his actions, God's history in his career, and God's compassion in his cross.'[25]

So does the Son of God 'become man'? Certainly the category 'becoming man' is alien to Jewish and originally Jewish-Christian thought and derives from the Hellenistic world. Yet this term, too, can be rightly understood in terms of a Jewish context. For it is quite wrong for the 'becoming man' to be fixed at the mathematical or mystical point of the conception ('the annunciation to Mary') or the birth of Jesus ('Christmas'). In the context of the history of the Jew Jesus, the Greek conceptual model of 'incarnation' must to some degree be buried. If we do this, then – as I have indicated – becoming man is rightly understood only in the light of the whole life and death and new life of Jesus.

So what does 'becoming man' mean, then? Becoming man means that in this person God's word, will and love took on human form. In all his speaking and proclamation, in all his actions, in his fate, in his whole person, the man Jesus did not act as God's double ('a second God'). Rather, he proclaimed, manifested and revealed the word and will of the one God. So perhaps even in a Jewish context the statement might be ventured that the one in whom, according to the witnesses, word and deed, teaching and life, being and action, fully coincide, is in human form God's word, God's will, God's image, God's Son. Certainly the issue here is a unity of Jesus with God. But even according to the christological councils there is no 'mixing' and 'joining', as Jews and Muslims fear, but – according to the New Testament – a unity of 'throne', of knowledge, of will, of Jesus' action with God, a unity of the revealing of God with and through Jesus. As the Gospel of John puts it, 'He who sees me sees the Father' (John 14.9).

In this original sense Jesus of Nazareth is the Word become flesh, God's Logos in person, God's wisdom in human form; and in this sense the contemporary Christian, too, can confess at the end of the second post-Christian millennium, 'Credo, I believe in Jesus Christ, God's only Son, our Lord.'

III

The Significance of Christ's Cross
and Death

If, then, one wanted to define something like a relationship between world views, without prior evaluation, the Christ of the Christians could be seen at the centre of a cross of co-ordinates in world history determined by the normative religious figures of humankind and the religions inspired by them. What do I mean by this?

1. In the cross of co-ordinates of the world religions

On the left branch of this cross of co-ordinates would stand the name Buddha, the prototype, as we saw, of the enlightened and the master of meditation: a symbolic figure from India to Japan for spiritual contemplation and interiorization and the monastic denial of the world in the community of an order. The Buddha – the very model for a life according to the Eightfold Path which leads to the transcending of suffering and to Nirvana.

On the right branch of the cross would be the name Confucius, the prototype of the Far Eastern sage, who stands for an ethic which exerts its influence throughout the world from Peking to Tokyo and from Seoul to Taipeh, wherever people can read Chinese script. Kung Fu-tzu – the symbolic figure for a persistent morality in family and society, renewed in the spirit and the ritual of an ideal primal time, guarantor of a moral world order, the very model of a life in harmony among human beings and between human beings and nature.

At the top of the cross we would read the name Moses, from

whom Jesus, like all Israelites, stems: Moses – the prototype of the prophet, the powerful symbolic figure for the Torah, for the unconditional validity of the written instructions of God which have then increasingly undergone human development. Moses – the very model for Jews everywhere of a life in accordance with God's instructions, God's law, in this world and precisely in this way a summons to a moral control of the world.

At the bottom would stand the name of Muhammad, who sees himself as a prophet very much in line with Moses and indeed with Jesus the Messiah, as the conclusion, the confirmatory 'seal', of all previous prophets. From Morocco to Indonesia, from Central Asia to the Horn of Africa, he is regarded as *the* prophet, the symbolic figure of a religion which also seeks totally to penetrate the sphere of society and aims to conquer the world with a view to setting up theocratic states. Muhammad – the very model of a life in accordance with the Qur'an, God's original and final revelation on the way to world judgment and paradise.

It should have become clear how irreplaceable and non-interchangeable are these representatives of the three great river systems of the high religions, which have their origin in quite different regions of the world:
– the Semitic river system, which has a prophetic character: Moses and Muhammad;
– the Indian river system, which has a mystical character: Buddha and Krishna;
– Far Eastern river system, which has the character of wisdom: Kung Fu-tzu and Lao-tzu.

These are no more-or-less chance possibilities, but representatives of a few basic religious positions or, better, basic options. For here people have to choose: with all respect for other ways, one cannot go along all of them at once. The ways are too different, even if today, it is to be hoped, they can often come closer to one another and may at some time meet somewhere in a hidden goal.

Those who choose discipleship of Jesus Christ as their way of life – and faith is a choice of unconditional, unshakable trust – choose a figure who is different from all these. Jesus Christ is:
– unlike the mystic who closes his eyes and ears in the spirit of Indian inwardness and solitude;

– unlike the enlightened sage in the spirit of Far Eastern harmony and humanity;

– unlike the charismatic proclaimer of the law and leader of the exodus in the spirit of a Near Eastern-Semitic religion of faith and hope;

– unlike the battle-tried prophet and military leader in the spirit of a victorious Arab belief in one God.

So this Christ is radically different, indeed for some people almost terrifyingly different, when we recall his picture that we have already brought to mind in comparison with that of the smiling Buddha on the lotus blossom: as the picture of the sufferer *par excellence*.

2. *The image of the sufferer* par excellence

For about a thousand years ago people did not dare to paint the picture of the suffering Jesus realistically. In the first centuries there was still an awareness of the monstrosity, indeed the absurdity, of what the Christian message asked of the world: to see one who came to his end on the tree of shame as Messiah, Christ, Son of God! And to see the cross of torture – this most abhorrent of all instruments of execution and deterrence – as a sign of life, salvation and victory! Whatever experts on symbols, psychotherapists and esoterics from the history of religion may want to read out of or into the symbolism of the cross, the cross of Jesus was primarily a brutal historical fact (hence Pontius Pilate also found his way into the Creed!) and had nothing to do with life, wholeness and true humanity – absolutely nothing. A man like the apostle Paul, who was at home in two worlds, the Jewish and the Hellenistic, was quite clear what he was asking of his contemporaries with his 'word of the cross': to the Greeks 'foolishness' and to the Jews 'a stumbling block'.[26] This was of course felt even more strongly in the Rome of the Caesars: what was being said of this man from Nazareth must have seemed a bad joke, quite literally a dumb, stupid, asinine message. That is precisely what is indicated by the first pictorial representation of the crucified Jesus that we have, a caricature scratched on a wall above the Palatine, the imperial residence in Rome, some time in the third century. It represents the suffering figure on the cross, but it has an ass's head and under it the graffito 'Alexamenos worships his God'.

Moreover it is hardly surprising that in the first three centuries of Christianity, while there are portrayals of Christ for example as a beardless, young, good shepherd, there is no portrayal of the crucified Christ, and that the cross came to be used as a symbol and a pictorial theme only after the shift that came with Constantine, first appearing on sarcophagi. The earliest portrayals of the crucifixion that we have come from the fifth century: one on an ivory plaque now in the British Museum, and the other on a wooden door of the Basilica Santa Sabina in Rome. But in both instances any expression of suffering is avoided: Christ appears in the attitude of the victor or at prayer. Even in the early Middle Ages and the Romanesque period the portrayal of Christ is marked throughout by restraint and reverence; the royal crown adorns not only the judge of the world but also the one who rules on the cross, even if people now dare to depict him increasingly in large sculpture.

It was only in High Gothic and the early Renaissance that the figure of Christ again lost its hieratic strictness in favour of noble humanity. Under the influence of the mysticism of suffering of Bernard of Clairvaux and Francis of Assisi, the suffering of Christ was now accentuated. But it was late Gothic which first made the suffering of the crucified Christ the dominant theme. Whereas for Fra Angelico, the Florentine Dominican monk of the early Italian Renaissance, the Christ still suffers in silent beauty, north of the Alps the sufferer was now increasingly depicted in the style of crass realism, with the crown of thorns on his head. And whereas the Italian high Renaissance, philosophically influenced by Neoplatonism and socially supported by the upper classes, depicts Christ as the prototype of the ideal man, German late Gothic, which grew far more out of the religious struggles of the individual and the collapse of society, depicts him as a scourged, tortured, broken, dying man of grief.

But none of the impressive representations of the crucified figure from this period surpasses one painted by an artist who has remained a quite unknown personality right down to the present day and whose real name was only rediscovered in the twentieth century: the crucifixion by Mathis Gothardt-Neithardt, called

Matthias Grünewald (c.1470-1528). On the eve of the Reformation of 1512-1515, when Germany was richer in artistic talent than ever before, on his winged altar at Isenheim, a powerful 'book' of proclamation which can be 'leafed through' over the altar, Grünewald put into pictures important statements from the Apostles' Creed. To some extent for working days, when the 'book' remained closed, he created a portrayal of the crucifixion of Jesus. It has shattering power, so that Grünewald's crucified Christ became the embodiment of boundless suffering.

This painting of the passion has only four figures beside the cross. To the right below the cross – from the observer's perspective – is John the Baptist, almost unmoved and steadfast, who points to the suffering figure with an index finger stretched out in a commanding way (Christocentricity in painting, so to speak, which is why this particular picture adorned Karl Barth's study; for Barth the innocent small white sacrificial lamb at the Baptist's feet with the golden cross, whose blood flows into the eucharistic chalice – a symbol for the sacrament – was of course less important).

Left of the cross is Jesus' mother, with wan, rigid face and corpse-white robe, her hands outstretched to her son in prayer yet near to helplessness, supported only by the grieving compassionate beloved disciple, painted wholly in red. And finally, kneeling before the cross, with sumptuous clothes and colouring and long blonde hair, her hands stretched upwards, is Mary of Magdala, the symbolic figure of the desperate struggle of the individual over God, which is provoked by this fiasco.

These few accompanying figures make the larger-than-life Christ stand out even more: his fingers are convulsively stretched out and bent, almost the most painful thing about this man of grief, and his feet are pierced by an over-large nail. His whole distorted body, covered in wounds, hangs down heavily. His head, additionally tortured by a crown of jagged thorns, has sunk on his breast. His lips, after the cry of godforsakeness, appear open, bloodless and rigid. Here is unprecedented passion preaching for educated and illiterate alike.

'Enough! too much suffering!' With such thoughts some contemporaries in the Museum Unterlinden in Colmar will turn away from this picture of torture and shame terrified, even repulsed:

'One can also exaggerate suffering . . .' But – there is no exaggeration in this picture, and anyone who talks like this does not know who had prayed in front of this crucified figure in Grünewald's time, there at the monastery of Isenheim. Not just the canons, in front in the choir stalls with all the other personnel, but, separated from them because of the danger of contact and infection, the poorest of the poor. Tormented, crushed together and disfigured, they looked through the great uprights of the screen, beyond the priest, towards their suffering Lord. These were people with leprosy, inflicted by the scourge, the 'burning suffering', the 'brand of hell', whose deformities of face, finger, skin and joints were not dissimilar to those of Grünewald's Christ. They prayed before this crucified figure. Even in the late Middle Ages, lepers were inexorably cast out of human society, often disinherited, and frequently even declared dead. Already around 1200 there were around 20,000 leprosaries for the lifelong isolation of lepers in Europe, one of them attached to the Antonite Monastery in Isenheim, in the hospital chapel of which Grünewald's altar used to stand.

'But we have this behind us; that is all the pious, gruesome Middle Ages,' exclaim today's contemporaries who have turned away from the crucified Christ. 'The Reformation already did away with the pictures and often even with the cross in the church, and our optimistic Enlightenment went one better. They were more aware than we are of how much mischief has been caused in the church with the cross – and still is, down to the present day.'

Indeed, I cannot dispute that it is bitter: unfortunately it is this deepest and strongest element in Christianity that has been brought more and more into disrepute by those 'pious' people who, as the pastor's son Nietzsche mocked, 'crept', bent, to the cross as 'mystifiers and mutterers and stay-at-homes', and having become old and cold have lost all 'morning boldness'.[27]

So in present-day terminology, 'creeping to the cross' means something like giving in, not trusting oneself, surrendering, bowing one's back dumbly, cringing, being dominated, subservient. And 'bearing one's cross' means surrendering oneself, humbling oneself, creeping away, not saying a word, keeping one's fist in one's pocket . . . The cross, a sign of weaklings and cowards in the church, where some hierarchs with precious crosses on their breasts attempt to justify as 'the cross willed by God' repression which they have inflicted upon themselves, like celibacy and discrimination against women and indeed blows of fate of every kind, and even the undesired blessing of children.

But does taking up one's cross mean all this? No, truly no. It has to be said quite firmly that according to the New Testament taking up one's cross does not mean accepting supervision; it doesn't even simply mean cultic worship or mystical contemplation; it does not mean esoteric-symbolic self-discovery by bringing the unconscious to consciousness, nor does it mean the literal ethical imitation of Jesus' way of life, which cannot be imitated at all now. Taking up one's cross does not mean taking up Christ's cross, but simply the cross of one's own life, which no one knows better than the person involved. This of course includes what Romano Guardini calls 'acceptance of oneself' and Carl Jung 'one's shadow'. Taking up one's cross means going one's own way in the risk of one's own situation and uncertainty about the future – of course following the direction of the one whose way has gone before, and to whom John the Baptist's finger points.

And there it is not enough, as in our Creed (or even on the Isenheim altar), as it were to leap from Christmas right over the whole public life of Jesus, his proclamation and his conduct, to Good Friday. The traditional Creed – and this is what wide-awake Christians among contemporaries particularly miss – does not say a single word about Jesus' message and life. To understand why Jesus of Nazareth had to *die*, we must understand how he *lived*. To understand why he had to die *this death*, we must have understood something of the time in which he lived. And to have some idea why he had to die *so early*, we must have an intimation who he was, what he stood for and against whom he spoke and fought. It is hardly possible to understand Jesus rightly without the political, social and religious situation of his time.

3. A political revolutionary?

Whatever may be disputed among Jewish and Christian scholars, there is agreement that Jesus was not a man of the Jewish establishment. He was not a Sadducee; he was neither a priest nor a theologian. He was a 'layman'! He did not see his place among the ruling class and nowhere showed himself to be a conformist, an apologist for the *status quo* or a defender of law and order. As a Christian theologian one can only agree with the Jewish scholar Joseph Klausner when he says: 'Jesus and his disciples, who came not from the ruling and wealthy classes, but from the common people, and but slightly affected by the Sadducees. . . The Galilean carpenter and son of a carpenter and the simple fishermen who accompanied him . . . were as remote from Sadducaeanism as the highly-connected priests were from the simple-minded common people. The bare fact that the Sadducees denied the resurrection of the dead and did not develop the messianic idea must have alienated Jesus and his disciples.'[28]

However, the important question is: was Jesus therefore a political revolutionary, as a first group of Jewish interpreters assumes? Now the Gospels certainly show a very clear-sighted, resolute, unbending Jesus, who if need be was also militant and combative; in any case he was fearless. He said that he had come to cast fire on the earth. One had not to fear those who could only kill the body and do no more than that. A time of the sword, a time of the utmost distress and danger, was imminent. But it is also clear that Jesus was no preacher of violence. His answer to the use of violence in the Sermon on the Mount is negative all along the line. Moreover, at his arrest Jesus says, 'Put your sword back into its place: for all who take the sword will perish by the sword' (Matt.26.52). At his arrest Jesus himself was unarmed, defenceless, non-violent. And so the disciples, who were doubtless arrested with him as a group of political conspirators, were left unmolested.

But 'what about the cleansing of the Temple, which indeed is sometimes even interpreted as an occupation of the Temple?' Jesus certainly had the courage for symbolic provocation. The Nazarene was by no means as meek and mild as the 'Nazarenes' of the nineteenth century – no Grünewalds! – used to paint him.

But according to the sources we cannot talk of an occupation of the Temple: in that case the Roman cohorts from the Antonia citadel would have intervened immediately, and the passion story would have taken a different course. No, according to the sources we have an expulsion of the merchants and money-changers: a symbolic intervention, an individual prophetic provocation, which amounts to a partisan demonstration: against the marketing and the hierarchy and profiteers who made a profit from it, and for the holiness of the place, which was to be a place of prayer. This action in the Temple was possibly connected with a threat about the destruction of the Temple and its rebuilding in this end-time. Such a religious provocation would doubtless also have been a blatant provocation to the clerical hierarchy and presumably also those circles in the city which had a financial interest in the pilgrimage business and further development of the Temple. Evidently it played an important, though by no means exclusive, role in the later condemnation of the Nazarene.

However, to make the point once again: there can be no question of a Zionist messianic revolution, which some Jewish scholars conjecture:

– Did Jesus perhaps call for a tax boycott? Hardly! 'Render to Caesar what is Caesar's!' (Matt.22.21) was his answer, and that is no call to refuse to pay tax. But conversely, of course, that means, 'Do not give to Caesar what is God's! Just as the currency belongs to Caesar, so human beings belong to God.'

– Did Jesus proclaim a national war of liberation? No: he clearly accepted invitations to dinner with the worst collaborators with the occupying power, and sometimes he presented the national enemies, the Samaritans, who were hated almost more than the Gentiles, as examples.

– Did Jesus then propagate the class struggle? How? He certainly did not divide people into friends and foes, as did so many militants of his time!

– Did Jesus abolish the law for the sake of revolution? No, he was a charismatic healer of the sick and he wanted to help, to heal, whomever he could. He wanted no happiness forced on the people in accordance with the will of some activists. First the kingdom of God, and then everything else will be added!

So Jesus' message of the kingdom of God did not culminate in an appeal to bring in the better future by force. Those who take the sword will perish by the sword. His message aims at a renunciation of violence. Do not resist the evil one; do good to those who hate us; bless those who curse us; pray for those who persecute us; free from their demons those who are tormented, anxious, blocked, psychosomatically sick. In this sense Jesus was a 'revolutionary', whose demands were fundamentally more radical than those of the political revolutionaries and transcended the alternatives of established order and socio-political revolution. Thus, rightly understood, in the goodness which he put into practice Jesus was more revolutionary than the revolutionaries:

– Healing and comfort instead of violation and wounding.
– Unconditional forgiveness instead of hitting back.
– Readiness for suffering instead of the use of violence.
– Blessing for the peacemakers instead of songs of hatred and revenge.
– Love of enemies instead of annihilation.

'But doesn't that mean,' it may now be asked, 'that Jesus was the advocate of a piety which turns its back on the world, indeed of a monastic asceticism?' The question must be answered in view of the fact that pseudo-scholars have constantly engaged in wild speculations in this connection.

4. An ascetic and monk?

Since the middle of this century it has been known that there were Jewish monks at the time of Jesus, in the monastery of Qumran by the Dead Sea. And from the time of the historian Flavius Josephus it has been known that 'pious people' (Aramaic *ḥasidyya*, Hebrew *ḥasidim*), now called Essenes, lived apart from the world in the villages (and in individual instances even in the cities). In the hey-day of Qumran scholarship there was a constant concern to find connections between Qumran and John the Baptist (which are possible) and even between Qumran and Jesus, but this has proved to be an increasingly improbable hypothesis. Neither the Qumran community nor the Essene movement are so much as mentioned in the New Testament writings, and conversely there is no mention of the name of Jesus in the Qumran writings (the publication of which has been delayed by ambitious, petty-minded specialists, and not, as a journalistic work claims, because of dangerous new texts).

It was Albert Schweitzer, that great scholar and later 'doctor of the primeval forest', who, as an academic theologian, once pointed out to middle-class liberal theologians that the Gospels do not present Jesus as a figure who conforms to society. During his public activity Jesus led an insecure itinerant life; for his family he was more of a 'drop-out', whom his mother and brothers wanted to get back home because he was 'crazy'. Jesus was also unmarried, a fact that has constantly seduced the imagination of novelists, film directors and musical composers to uninteresting and unverifiable hypotheses.

So was Jesus a follower of or a sympathizer with this monastic community? No, Jesus was not a highly spiritual member of an order or an ascetic monk. What distinguished him? Much:

– Jesus did not live in seclusion from the world: his activity was quite public, in the villages and cities, in the midst of human society. He even made contact with the socially disreputable, with those who were 'unclean' according to the law and written off by Qumran, even with lepers, and caused scandal as a result. Purity of heart seems to have been more important to him than any precepts of external purity.

– Unlike the Qumran monks, Jesus did not preach any division of humanity: it was not his concern to classify people as sons of light and sons of darkness, good and evil – a priori and from the beginning. Everyone has to repent, and anyone can repent; forgiveness is offered to all and a new beginning made possible.

– Jesus did not lead an ascetic life; he was not a zealot for the law, like members of the Essene and Qumran orders. He did not stipulate abstinence for the sake of abstinence, or any special ascetic disciplines. Rather, he joined in, ate and drank with his followers, and was invited to banquets. Compared with the Baptist, he evidently incurred the charge of being a glutton and a winebibber. He made an unforgettable impression on his disciples, not by baptism, but by the supper that he had with them under the threat of his arrest. For him marriage was not something that made people unclean but the will of the Creator. Renunciation of marriage was voluntary, and he did not impose a law of celibacy on anyone. Even the renunciation of all material possessions was not necessarily a condition of discipleship (if people did not want to join him in his itinerant life).

– Jesus did not lay down any religious rule: he turned upside down the hierarchical system which was customary in the religious orders then as now: the lowliest are to be the highest and the highest the servants of all. Subordination has to be mutual, for the common good. And for that there is no need of a novitiate, of promises upon entry, of vows, of oaths of loyalty. Jesus did not call for any regular pious practices, any long prayers, any distinctive clothing, any ritual baths. What marked him out was a lack of regulations, a matter-of-factness, a spontaneity and a freedom which for Qumran would have been criminal. For Jesus, incessant praying did not mean an hour of prayer or an interminable liturgy but a human attitude of constant prayer which at all times looks to God for everything and at all times also has time for God.

But what is left – for then and for today? The answer is that the Jesus of history also stands in a cross of coordinates of different options within Judaism, which are significant even today: if Jesus did not want to subscribe to the establishment, but on the other hand did not want the political radicalism of a violent revolution either, and if finally he did not preach the apolitical radicalism of the pious who opted out of society, must not then a fourth option within Judaism have applied to him: the option of moral compromise, the harmonization of the demands of the law with the demands of everyday life? That had been the concept of the Pharisaism of the day. So the question is: was Jesus something like a Pharisee?

5. A pious Pharisee?

However, I can hear contemporaries, and truly not just Jewish contemporaries, saying: 'But today we know that the picture of the Pharisees in the Gospels is incorrect in many respects. Their picture has a priori been caricatured by the conflict which the young Christian community fought out with them in particular. Indeed they were also the only representatives of official Judaism left after the destruction of the Temple and the whole city of Jerusalem. They were now the main opponents of the young

Christian communities, the scapegoats for many things.' That is right. Today even in church documents one can find a call for rethinking about the Pharisees. The decisive concern of the Pharisees was to actualize the Torah as the obligatory word of God in the present. These were men who took God's cause with great seriousness and who made 'joy in the law' their basic attitude.

The name Pharisee means 'the separated'. And these 'separated' ones had two specific concerns: they wanted to take God's commandments with unconditional seriousness and to observe them with scrupulous exactitude. Indeed, starting from the conviction that Israel is a 'kingdom of priests and a holy people' (Ex.19.6), they wanted voluntarily to observe strictly the regulations on cleanness (and especially also those relating to tithes) which were binding only on the priests. But at the same time, as men (women played no part even in the Pharisaic movement) who were near to the people in quite a different way from the priests in the Temple, they wanted to make the law livable in everyday life by wise adaptation to the present: they wanted to define precisely how far one could go without sinning.

And what about Jesus? Didn't he have much in common with the Pharisees in particular? The relationship between Jesus and the Pharisees would need to be discussed very carefully, and I have done this in my book on *Judaism*. Christian interpreters of Jesus have all too tendentiously overlooked or neglected what Jesus has in common with the Pharisees, at the expense of Judaism. Like the Pharisees, Jesus lived among the people: he worked, discussed, and taught in synagogues as they did. Jesus had contacts with Pharisees, and according to Luke also ate and drank with them. Indeed, if we follow Jewish and Christian authors, some rabbinic parallels and analogies can be demonstrated to most of the verses of the Sermon on the Mount. No wonder, then, that most Jewish interpreters see Jesus as being close to the Pharisees. And indeed, as for the Pharisees, so for Jesus, the authority of Moses was not in question. It should never have been disputed that Jesus too did not want to abolish the Torah, to do away with it; he wanted to 'fulfil it' (Matt.5.17).

But we should remember that for Jesus to 'fulfil' – and this follows from the passages of the Sermon on the Mount which

come after this saying – means to deepen, concentrate and radicalize the law of God: in the light of its innermost dimension, namely God's basic purpose. Jesus is convinced that nothing may be read into the law or out of the law that contradicts this basic intent, the will of God – which is aimed at human well-being. Of course this relates particuarly to the halakhic part of the law, which with its words, commandments and legal statements makes up barely a fifth of the Pentateuch. In concrete, 'fulfil' means:
– to deepen the law by resolutely taking seriously the will of God in the law;
– to concentrate the law by combining love of God with love of neighbour: love as the nucleus and criterion of the law;
– to radicalize the law by extending love of neighbour beyond the other members of one's people also to enemies. And how? By boundless forgiveness, a renunciation of power and rights without asking anything in return, by service without superordination or subordination.

Pinchas Lapide may well be right about the rabbinical parallels and analogies to the Sermon on the Mount (and the preaching of Jesus generally) in saying that the Sermon on the Mount is as different from its Jewish parallels as a building is from the stones of the quarry from which it is built. That is the only explanation of the tremendous weight of its message, which has constantly put Christians themselves to shame, and which could even inspire people from a completely different cultural circle, like Mahatma Gandhi. It makes a difference whether three dozen sentences can be attested among three dozen different rabbis in three dozen passages in the Talmud or whether they are found and concentrated in only one. So it is not the individual statements made by Jesus which are not interchangeable, but his message as a whole. And the question is not whether love of God and love of neighbour can also already be found in the Hebrew Bible (indisputably they can!), but what role they have in the proclamation of the rabbi from Nazareth, what status they are given, and what conclusions are drawn from them.

In other words, there is not the least to be said against the Pharisees 'in themselves' and their real virtues. In particular the Pharisee cited as an example in the famous parable (Luke 18.9-14) is no hypocrite. He is an utterly honest, pious man who speaks pure truth. After all, he had done everything he was convinced the law required of him. The morals of the Pharisees were quite exemplary, and accordingly were respected by those who did not go as far as they did. So what is to be said against them?

But once again, was Jesus then simply a pious, a 'liberal' Pharisee? In details of daily life there are undeniable similarities, but in his whole religious basic attitude Jesus was different. We find no pride in his own achievements, his own righteousness, no contempt for the ordinary people (the *am-ha-aretz*) who knew nothing of the law. There is no exclusion of the unclean and the sinners, no strict doctrine of retribution. What then? Trust only in God's grace and mercy: 'God, be merciful to me a sinner!' (Luke 18.13). The poor publican, who has no achievements to show to God, is praised for his believing trust and not the Pharisee. This is justification of the sinner, on the basis of his faith.

No, on the basis of the authentic sources there is no getting round the fact that Jesus was certainly not a typical Pharisee with 'delight in the commandment' and casuistic exposition. It is wrong to compare individual statements out of context: the texts should be read in context. Do that, and it is possible to see how all the Gospels are in complete agreement in attesting that the 613 commandments and prohibitions of the law, which were so important to the Pharisees, were not what Jesus wanted to inculcate. Nowhere does he require his disciples to study the Torah. Nowhere does he seek to follow the Pharisees in building a 'hedge round the law' with regulations about how to carry it out, a protection to guarantee the observance of the commandments. Nowhere does he seek like them to extend the ideals of the cleanness and holiness of the priests in Temple service to the laity and their everyday practice.

In short, the basic attitude, the overall tendency, is different: compared with all the Pharisees, Jesus has astounding openness and laxity. Must it not have undermined the whole moral system for someone to show such solidarity with the unclean and sinners, indeed to sit at table with them? For the lost and dissolute son finally to have a better standing with his Father than the well-bred son who stays at home, indeed for the crooked tax-collector to fare better with God than the pious Pharisee, who really is not like other people, like liars and adulterers? Despite all the sympathy I have for rabbinic Judaism, at this point one must not disguise the facts, but must openly take account of the difference.

6. Not the usual scholastic disputes, but confrontation and conflict

Most Jewish and Christian interpreters of Jesus nowadays agree that Jesus, 'the greatest observer and critic of Pharisaic spirituality',[29] was not concerned with observing the Torah for its own sake, but with the well-being of actual individuals. His freer attitude to the law and his dealings with those who were ignorant of the law, or who broke it, thus led to serious confrontations. That is the unambiguous picture which is given to us by the authentic sources, the Gospels: Jesus specifically caused offence, scandal, not only by criticizing the Temple but by his different interpretation of the law, indeed his whole basic attitude. This applies above all to three problem fields which are still significant in Judaism:
- the regulations about cleanness;
- the regulations about fasting; and
- the Sabbath.

Does such a distinction help Jewish-Christian dialogue? I believe that such dialogue is most helped by sympathy, thorough research and intellectual honesty. For as a Christian ecumenist I passionately protest against the Christian isolation of Jesus from his Jewish roots. But conversely, I hope that Jewish ecumenists will also object to the levelling down of the message of Jesus among Jews – which has so long been repudiated in Judaism. Historically speaking, is it really enough to call Jesus a great Pharisee who, like other great Pharisees, had his own 'special material'? May we for the sake of friendship between Jews and Christians reduce Jesus' conflict and its fatal outcome to the level of the other disputes over interpretation within Pharisaic schools? Did Jesus of Nazareth die because of scholastic disputes? At any rate it was the Nazarene and none of the other 'liberal' rabbis who was drawn into a conflict which ended in death.

'But,' a contemporary asks here, 'aren't the conflicts in the framework of this cross of co-ordinates always on the horizontal level? What has become of the vertical? Where does God himself come into play with this Jesus?' Now if we follow the sources, these conflicts continually raised the question: 'With what right, with what authority, do you speak and do that?' This question of authority cannot be passed over, but must be discussed in its own right. It remains an urgent question:

7. In whose name?

What do you think of him? Who is he? One of the prophets? Or more? This question already runs through all the Gospels as a leading question. But even conservative Christian theologians today concede that Jesus did not proclaim himself, but the kingdom of God: 'Your kingdom come, your will be done' (Matt.6.10). He did not put his own role, person, dignity at the centre of his preaching.

That is also particularly true of the title Messiah. According to the Synoptic Gospels Jesus never used the designation Messiah or any other messianic title (except perhaps the ambiguous name 'Son of Man'). On this nowadays Christian and Jewish interpreters largely agree. The earliest evangelist Mark still treats Jesus' messiahship as a secret which is hidden from the public until it is finally confessed under the cross and proclaimed after Easter. Why? Only in the light of the Easter experience was it possible to see the whole Jesus tradition in a messianic light and thus introduce the explicit confession of Jesus as Messiah into the account of the story of Jesus. But Jesus' proclamation and practice in any case did not match the Jewish messianic expectations, which were so different, contradictory and mostly theo-political (even most rabbis expected a triumphant Messiah).

Now precisely because Jesus cannot adequately be 'grasped' with any of the current titles, precisely because the issue is not one of saying yes or no to a particular dignity, office or even a particular dogma, rite or law, the question put by the very first disciples becomes even sharper: who may he really have been? This great question about the mystery of his person remains to the present day. And the very avoidance of all 'titles' makes the riddle more profound.

Given Jesus' violent death, this riddle is posed in a special way. The death of Jesus cannot be separated from the question of his message and person. Here had appeared a man who in word and deed happily disregarded the hierarchy and its experts over cultic tabus, fasting practices and in particular demands of the sabbath commandment, which already at that time was in practice largely regarded as the chief commandment. And although the fact is also disputed by some Jewish interpreters, according to the Gospels, in free authority and against the prevailing teaching and practice which was the teaching and practice of the rulers, this Jesus had claimed an authority which made the scribes ask: 'How can this man speak like this? He blasphemes God' (Mark 2.7). But did he really blaspheme God?

The evidence to the contrary is unanimous. The Jew Jesus spoke on the basis of an experience of God, a union with God, indeed an immediacy to God which was unusual for a prophet. He thus acted on the basis of an unusual freedom, truthfulness and goodness when he preached the rule and will of God in confrontation with the rulers and did not simply accept the conditions of human domination:

– when he was open to all groups;
– when he was unwilling to deliver women (of whom there were many among his disciples!) over to the whim of their husbands in marriage;
– when he defended children against adults, the poor against the rich, the small against the great;
– when he even stood up for those with other religious beliefs, the politically compromised, the moral failures, those who had been sexually exploited, indeed even the lepers and those forced to the edge of society, and perhaps even – as the height of arrogance – promised 'sinners' forgiveness, something that was permitted only to the high priest on the Day of Atonement.

But the astounding thing is that nowhere does Jesus give grounds for his claim. Indeed, in the discussion on authority he refuses to give any grounds for it. He claims this authority, he acts on the basis of it, without appealing to a higher authority, with the prophetic 'Thus says the Lord!'. Here we do not have just an expert like the priests and the scribes, but one who proclaims God's will without any derivation and basis in word and action; who identifies himself with God's cause which is the human cause; who enters completely into this cause and so

79

becomes the highly personal advocate of God and human beings. That explains questions like this: was he not basically 'more than Jonah (and all the prophets)' (Matt.12.41; Luke 11.32), 'more than Solomon (and all the wisdom teachers)' (Matt.12.42; Luke 11.31)? According to the sources, the basis for the trial of Jesus must quite clearly be sought in this direction, regardless of whether or not at the time he was directly regarded as a 'messianic pretender' – and here the exegetes take different views.

But a contemporary in the know will have a burning question: 'Are the Jewish people now again to be made responsible for Jesus' death?' This question must be investigated in full awareness that the racist antisemitism of the National Socialists would not have been possible without the almost two thousand years of anti-Judaism in the churches, Catholic and Protestant alike, grounded in christology.

8. Who is to blame for Jesus' death?

Much remains uncertain about the trial of Jesus before the Jewish authorities. This may have been held before only a committee (composed predominantly of Sadducees) rather than the plenary session of the Sanhedrin; strikingly, the Pharisees are not mentioned in the accounts of the trial. Rather than pronouncing a formal death sentence, the body may have resolved simply to hand Jesus over to Pontius Pilate. Indeed, rather than a regular trial, perhaps there was only an interrogation to define the precise points of the charge – to be sent on to the Roman governor. It is somewhat improbable that the direct formal question whether Jesus was Messiah was the main charge, as that was not necessarily grounds for condemnation, and in any case the question whether Jesus was Son of God may be attributed to the later community.

'Many' charges are mentioned, but – a point which often fails to be noted – they are not cited, with one exception (the Temple!). They have to be inferred from the Gospels as a whole. And the evangelists have truthfully reported plenty of conflicts which cannot simply be explained as a back-projection of the controversy between the earliest church and the synagogue, but may have been some reflection of the historical conflict which had already broken out between the historical Jesus and the priestly-Sadducaean ruling classes.

For if we examine the Gospels without prejudice, the charges which point to some completely coherent basic attitude on the part of the accused can be summed up as follows:

– The Jew Jesus was a radical critic of the traditional religious practice of many pious Jews in particular.

– Jesus' protest action and prophecy against the trading in the Temple and thus against its priestly guardians and those who benefited from it in business seemed arrogant.

– Jesus' uncasuistic understanding of the Torah, the law, above all relating to the sabbath and the regulations for fasting and cleanness, focussed wholly on human beings, was provocative.

– Jesus' solidarity with ordinary people who were ignorant of the law and his dealings with notorious law-breakers were scandalous.

– Jesus' criticism of the ruling groups, to whom he was more than just a nuisance because of his numerous following among the people, was sweeping.

But whatever may have been the details of the trial – which can hardly be reconstructed satisfactorily – all the evangelists agree that Jesus was handed over to the Roman governor Pontius Pilate by the Jewish authorities and crucified in accordance with Roman practice: 'crucifixus sub Pontio Pilato', as it says in the Creed, stressing the historicity of the event. However, according to all the reports on Pilate, on whose governorship of Judaea (26-36 CE) all the sources pass a very negative verdict, the political term 'king of the Jews' (rex Iudaeorum) was the major factor. So Jesus ironically appeared as what he should not at all have been for the protesting Jewish authorities: the Messiah king. The inscription on the cross put there by Roman custom states the particular grounds for condemnation (causa damnationis). 'King of the Jews' could of course only be understood by the Romans in political terms: as the assumption of a royal title. And that was an infringement of Roman majesty (crimen laesae maiestatis). And indeed although Jesus, this preacher of non-violence, had never made such a political claim, it was natural for outsiders to put him in this category.

So what was the issue? If we follow the sources, in the case of

Jesus it was not a political revolt but religious provocation. This may have been the reason why Jewish authorities were at work from the start: behind the religious charge there was fundamentally a political charge. And according to the Gospels, this religious charge can only have had to do with Jesus' critical attitude to the law and the Temple, and to their representatives. As a purely political agitator, Jesus would presumably have sunk into oblivion even at that time, like others – apart from the name. But as a religious figure with his message and his free, truthful and generous conduct, he had incurred the charge of stirring up the people against the political and religious authorities. As we have heard, from the standpoint of the prevailing interpretation of the law and Temple religion the Jewish hierarchy would not necessarily have had to take action against a messianic pretender or a pseudo-Messiah. But things were different in the case of a false teacher, a lying prophet, a blasphemer, someone who led the people astray. In this perspective, at that time the cruel death of Jesus could have been seen as a well-deserved fate: law and order have won. As the one hanging on the tree of shame, Jesus appeared to be the accursed of God.

There is no doubt that the trial of Jesus was a 'transformation of the Jewish charge, relating to religious transgressions, into the political charge of high treason'.[30]

That means that:

– the political charge that Jesus had striven for political power, had called on people to refuse to pay taxes to the occupying forces and incited unrest, and had thus understood himself as the political-messiah king of the Jews, was according to the sources a false charge.

– But Jesus, the religious trouble-maker, was executed as a political messianic pretender and revolutionary, i.e. as a militant opponent of Roman power. For Pilate this was a plausible charge, since, in the circumstances of the time, political unrest, rebels and false messiahs were nothing unusual. That means that the religious trouble-maker was condemned as a political revolutionary, though he was nothing of the sort.

So who is to blame for Jesus' death? The correct historical answer can only be: not 'the' Jews or 'the' Romans, but particular Jewish and Roman authorities were each entangled in this case in their own way. Therefore in view of the fearful effect that this has had in anti-Judaism, it must be said:

– As 'people', 'the' Jews did not already reject Jesus at that time; there should never have been any talk of the collective guilt of the Jewish people of the time (why not also of the Roman people?).

– It is even more absurd to make the Jewish people of today collectively guilty. Casting blame for the death of Jesus on the present Jewish nation was and is perverse: it has brought infinite suffering on this people in past centuries, and was even a contributory cause to Auschwitz.

Moreover, in view of a monstrous history of guilt on the part of Christians, who were brought up on the charge that 'the Jews' were murderers of Christ, even murderers of God, the Second Vatican Council has finally brought clarity: 'Even though the Jewish authorities and those who followed their lead pressed for the death of Christ, neither all Jews indiscriminately at that time, nor Jews today, can be charged with the crime committed during his passion.'[31] Or positively, anyone who is for Jesus cannot, for theological reasons alone, be against his people, the Jews.

What is decisive for understanding the passion of Jesus today is not a look back into the distant past but a look on the part of each individual at himself or herself, as still happens in the unsurpassed passion music of Johann Sebastian Bach. Then the death of Jesus is no longer a question to the Jewish people of the time, but a question to each individual Christian today, whether we are not still crucifiying Jesus by our behaviour and where we would have stood at that time;

– with Pontius Pilate, who denied the truth for the sake of opportunity;

– or with the hierarchs Annas and Caiaphas, who sacrificed the well-being of an individual for the sake of a religious law or paragraph;

– or with Peter, who in the hour of need denied his friend and master, or even with Judas, who betrayed him;

– or with the Roman cohort, which – orders are orders – was capable of any meanness and inhumanity;

– or among the women, who from Pilate's wife to Mary Magdalene stood at his side and remained loyal to him.

So after all that we have heard, is that 'bringing home' of Jesus to Judaism of which Jewish authors speak possible today? No and yes. Perhaps not home to the religious law, the halakah, which, having been relativized by Jesus, retreated into the background and was no longer regarded in its totality as unconditionally necessary for salvation by those who later believed in Jesus as the Christ – an attitude which is now shared by many Jews. But certainly home to the Jewish people, the permanently chosen people, who had for long rejected, indeed for long had to reject, the rabbi from Nazareth, not least because of the Christians. Today the Nazarene appears as a 'brother' (to use Martin Buber's term), even to many Jews, indeed as the primal figure of the Jewish people, persecuted in the world and condemned to unspeakable suffering. And if he returned today, as in Dostoievsky's 'Grand Inquisitor', whom would he have to fear the most? Who would more readily accept him, the synagogue or the church?

Dostoievsky's 'Grand Inquisitor', or better his chapter on Jesus, is, however, an accusation not only against the church but centrally against God himself – only too understandable in the face of the suffering, in the face of all the natural catastrophes, all the absurdities of life, all the orgies of evil, all the streams of tears and blood, all the murdered innocents. It is an accusation crying to heaven against that divine primal principle which is responsible for order and harmony in this world, whether one calls it Heaven, Tao, Lord in the Highest, the Great Ultimate, Godhead or God; that God whom Leibniz hoped to justify in the face of evil in his 'theodicy' or 'justification'. It is an accusation and revolt against God which Dostoievsky's Ivan Karamazov formulated more sharply than anyone, from the patient Job to the frivolous Voltaire, with his reference to innocently tortured children and his request to the Creator to be allowed to return his entrance ticket to a world which is so discordant. Is that the utter end?

'No,' Alyosha replies to his brother Ivan, 'You have forgotten him.' And there follows Ivan's great story of the Grand Inquisitor, perhaps the most fearful charge against a church which suppresses freedom, but which, as Alyosha perceptively remarks, in reality marvellously 'praises Jesus' who has brought freedom. But particularly in the light of the crucified Jesus, the question of God poses itself once again in a most radical way. Precisely in the light of Jesus of Nazareth, who lived in an unprecedented relationship

84

of trust in God, precisely in the light of him, the question must be asked: what kind of a God is it who allows such crosses – from Golgotha to Auschwitz? And also my own quite personal cross?

'When are you going to talk about God and suffering?', a contemporary asked me, this time in the figure of a woman student whom I did not know, immediately after my lecture on the first article of faith, belief in God the Father almighty. And I grant that this question has pursued me ever since. How much suffering can be concealed by such a question? And what answer is one to give to it? One thing at any rate is clear: the question of the historical causes of the crucifixion, which we have been investigating so far, automatically raises the question: is there not only the 'brute fact' of the cross, but also a 'meaning' of the cross? Can we, may we – as a comforting answer – perhaps speak of a 'crucified God'?

9. A crucified God?

After the Second World War, Christian theologians, referring to a remark by Dietrich Bonhoeffer, often sought to tackle the problems of the cross by assuming a 'suffering God'. God is 'weak and powerless in the world' and that is precisely the way, the only way, in which he is with us and helps us . . . only the "suffering God" can help'.[32] In respect of the Holocaust, individual theologians have concluded from this that the 'inexpressible suffering of the six million is also the voice of the suffering God'.[33] Yet other theologians have thought that they could deal with the problems of suffering in a highly speculative way by means of a history of suffering which is played out dialectically within the Trinity between God and God, indeed by God against God.

But we need to be cautious: taught by the great Jewish-Christian tradition and with awareness of Hegel's problematical thought-model, we do well to be reserved towards such speculations about a 'suffering God', a 'crucified God',[34] even a 'death of God',[35] which are inspired more by Hegel than by the Bible. For Jews and Muslims they have always been impossible to follow and are so today also for quite a few critical Christians. As if christological speculations and conceptual manipulations of the concept of God could really put the immense and especially the innocent, meaningless suffering of human life, this human history, and finally also the Holocaust on a 'higher plane' and deal with it that way. Today Jewish theology at any rate is attempting to respond theologically to the challenge of the Holocaust without such christological reflections. And for Christian theologians, too – for all God's 'humanity', or more precisely loving-kindness (*philanthropia*, Titus 3.4), which appears specifically in Christ Jesus – there must at any rate be no levelling down of transcendence, no sell-out of the divinity of God, not even in the face of such incomprehensible suffering and grief.

A look at scripture may sober up such speculative boldness. According to the Old Testament, people keep crying to God in trust that God will hear their cries and weeping, but their crying, suffering and dying does not simply become the crying, suffering and dying of God. Granted, in anthropomorphic language the Hebrew Bible sometimes attributes the whole range of human feelings and attitudes to God: anger, complaint and pain at the conduct of his people, and also time and again patience and the withholding of his anger. But nowhere is the difference between God and human beings done away with, nor is human suffering and pain simply declared to be the suffering and pain of God and thus transfigured. Nowhere does God's Godliness become ungodliness, his faithfulness unfaithfulness, his reliability unreliability, his divine mercy human pitifulness. For the Hebrew Bible, though human beings fail, God does not fail; when human beings die, God does not die also. For 'I am God and not man, the holy one in your midst', states Hosea 11.9 against any humanization of God, although at this very point as elsewhere there is anthropomorphic talk of God's 'compassion' on his people.

Also according to the New Testament, Jesus, the Son of God, cries to God his Father because he believes that he has been forsaken by God in the depths of his suffering. But nowhere does God cry to God, nowhere is God himself weak, helpless, suffering, crucified or even dead. If one identifies human suffering so much with God that it is also God's suffering; if the cry of human beings becomes the cry of God, then would not the consequence also be that human sins (the crimes of the SS butchers and others) become the sins of God himself?

No, as a Christian theologian thinking biblically one cannot avoid the sobering observation that the message, the word of the cross, is according to Paul only weakness and folly for those who do not believe, and for those who do believe it is God's power, God's wisdom (cf. I Cor.1.18-31). This is a paradox, but not a contradiction, and it is important for Jewish-Christian dialogue: according to the whole of the New Testament, in line with the Old and against all Gnostic and Kabbalistic speculations, on the cross of Jesus Christ it was not simply God who was crucified: the God, *ho theos, Deus pater omnipotens* (far less, of course, God's Holy Spirit). How else could the crucified Jesus, forsaken by God, have been able to cry out to God, 'My God, my God, why have you forsaken me?'(Mark 15.34)?

In other words: the cross is not the symbol of the 'suffering', 'screaming God', indeed 'the symbol of God suffering the distress of death', but the symbol of humanity suffering the distress of death. And the Hebrew Bible later provided a pattern of interpretation for assimilating this tremendous event: the model is not a suffering God but
– the prophet commissioned by God but persecuted by human beings;
– the servant of God who suffered innocently and vicariously for the sins of many;
– the sacrificial lamb which symbolically takes away the sins of humankind.

No, on the cross, as this is understood throughout the New Testament, it is not God himself (*ho theos*), the Father, who died, but God's Messiah and Christ, God's Image, Word and Son. At a very early stage the church rightly condemned an unbiblical 'patripassianism', the view that God the Father himself suffered.[36] Jewish theology rightly protests against a sadistic, cruel picture of God, according to which a bloodthirsty God calls for the sacrifice of his Son. I hope that Christian theology will no less emphatically protest against a masochistic, tolerant understanding of God according to which a weak God has to torture himself to resurrection by suffering and death if he is not to suffer eternally.

Even as theologians, let us make no mistake about it: taken by itself the cross is a clear fiasco, which cannot be turned into any kind of mystery. It is an unprecedented abandonment of the one sent by God, by both human beings and by God. To this degree we must agree with Hans Blumenberg when he seeks to read out of Jesus' cry of lament over his godforsakenness the 'failure of God' in his work, God's 'self-sublation'. If we concentrate solely on the death of Jesus on the cross, it is virtually impossible to contradict Blumenberg. But Johann Sebastian Bach's *St Matthew Passion*, which Blumenberg uses in his interpretation, ends, like the Gospels themselves, with the certainty of resurrection and redemption and the 'covenant of peace' between human beings and God.[37] Only in the light of the resurrection of Jesus to life can God's hidden presence be accepted in faith after the event, in his manifest absence. This cannot be understood speculatively in the sense of a self-resurrection of God. For again, according to the whole of the New Testament, the raising to new life is not proclaimed of God but only of Jesus, the Son. But who is the subject of this raising? Obviously God himself (*ho theos*), who is a God of the living and not of the dead: the 'Father'. 'He' – and Paul says this not of God but of Christ the Son of God – 'was crucified in weakness, but lives in the power of God' (II Cor. 13.4).

Indeed, only in this way, by the acceptance of this Son into God's eternal life, does God show himself to be near in solidarity with believers as he is with this only Son (and thus with all sons and daughters), even in extreme suffering, in forsakenness and in dying: as the one who also shares in our grief and our suffering (merited or unmerited), as the one who is also affected by our suffering and by all injustice, compassionate in a hidden way and precisely in this way right to the end the infinitely gracious and powerful God.

This is the most I may say on the basis of scripture about the question of God and suffering. But on the basis of this conviction of faith, is it possible to talk about the most difficult test case, which affects Jews and Christians together most deeply? Any reflective contemporary will ask: 'Is God also in the hell of Auschwitz?'

10. A test case for the question of theodicy: God in Auschwitz?

Having been constantly preoccupied for decades with all the attempts at theodicy, I can confidently say quite bluntly that there seems to me to be no theoretical answer to the problem of theodicy. On the basis of an attitude of faith only one thing can be said:
– If God exists, then God was also in Auschwitz! Even in this death factory, believers of different religions and confessions held on to the conviction that despite everything, God lives.
– At the same time, however, the believer has to concede that there is no answer to the question 'How could God have been in Auschwitz without preventing Auschwitz?'

Despite all pious apologetic we must concede soberly that any theologians who seek to get behind the mystery, the mystery of God himself, will at best discover there their own theolgoumena, their own little theological discoveries. Neither the Hebrew Bible nor the New Testament explains to us how the good, just and powerful God – in the end we cannot give up any of these attributes if we are still to talk about *God*! – how God in this world could have allowed such immeasurable suffering to have happened in things small (but what is 'small' here?) and great (indeed excessively great). How could have God 'shared in seeing' that Auschwitz was made possible? How could God have 'looked on' when the gas streamed out and the cremation ovens were burning?

Or should I simply console myself over all the suffering of the Holocaust with the classical theological formula that God does not will suffering, but does not not will it either; rather, God simply lets it happen: *permittit*, 'allows it'? But does that solve all the riddles? No, it did not solve them yesterday any more than it does today. But there is a counter-question: should we then simply eliminate this primal human problem? On the basis of what new insights, on the basis of what new experiences? It does not need to have been the Holocaust in particular. Sometimes a failure at work, an illness, the loss, betrayal or death of just one person is enough to cast us into despair. That is what happened to the American Rabbi Harold S.Kushner. Because he lost a child by a tragic illness, he wrote a book whch went on to become a bestseller: *When Bad Things Happen to Good People*.[38] His suggested solution was to abandon the notion of God's omnipotence. Others find the thought 'when good things happen to bad people' just as trying and would very much like to deny God's goodness and justice. But neither is a way out of the dilemma. We have heard that 'omnnipotence' is an attribute of God which can be misunderstood. But a God robbed of all power would cease to be God. And the idea that the God of the Bible were cruel and arbitrary rather than gracious and just is even more intolerable.

For better or for worse, we have to put up with the fact that the problem is not solved by either any over-hasty negations or any highly-speculative affirmations. What a presumption of the human spirit this is, whether it comes in the guise of theological scepticism, philosophical metaphysics, the idealistic philosophy of history or trinitarian speculation! Perhaps people will learn from this to understand the arguments of Epicurus, Bayle, Feuerbach or Nietzsche against such theodicy less as blasphemy of God than as mockery of human beings and especially of the arrogance of theologians. On this most difficult question, a theology of silence would seem to me to be better. 'If I were to know him, I would be him', goes an old Jewish saying. And some Jewish theologians who prefer to dispense with an ultimate justification of God in the face of all suffering simply quote the terse word of scripture which follows the report of the death of Aaron's two sons who were killed by the divine fire: 'And Aaron held his peace.'[39]

Indeed, atheists and sceptics are right: none of the great spirits of humanity – whether Augustine or Thomas or Calvin, Leibniz or Hegel – has solved the basic problem. Kant wrote his *On the Failure of all Philosophical Attempts at a Theodicy* in 1791, when in Paris people were thinking of doing away with God and replacing him with the goddess Reason.

But I must also put a question back to my sceptical contemporaries: is then, say, atheism the solution? An atheism which would see its Faustian pledge in Auschwitz? Is Auschwitz the rock of atheism? Does godlessness explain the world better? Its misery and its grandeur? Does it explain the world as it now is? Can unbelief bring consolation in innocent, incomprehensible, meaningless suffering? As if all unbelieving reason did not also have its limits in such suffering! As if Auschwitz were not largely the action of god-less criminals? No, here the anti-theologian is no better off than the theologian. 'So how can we cope with suffering?' This is a question which I cannot leave unanswered.

11. Meaningless suffering cannot be understood theoretically, but must be endured in trust

There is no avoiding the sobering acknowledgment that if neither a theological nor an anti-theological 'theory' explains suffering, then another basic attitude is called for. It is my insight, which has grown over the decades and to which so far I have not found a convincing alternative, that suffering – excessive, innocent, meaningless suffering, both individual and collective – cannot be understood theoretically, but can only be lived through. For Christians and Jews there is only a practical answer to the problem of theodicy. What is that? In this question both Jews and Christians may point to different, yet interconnected, traditions.

In extreme meaningless suffering, Jews, and also Christians, have in view the figure of Job, which indicates two things: in the last resort God is and remains incomprehensible to human beings, and yet human beings are given the possibility of showing an unshakable, unconditional trust in this incomprehensible God, rather than resignation or despair. In the light of Job they can trust that God also respects the human protest against suffering and finally becomes manifest as the creator of human beings, who redeems them from suffering.

For Christians – and why not ultimately also for Jews? – in extreme suffering, over and above the figure of Job (who in the last resort is fictitious), there shines out the truly historical figure of the suffering and dying 'servant of God' (cf. Isa.52.13-53.12), the man of grief from Nazareth. Grünewald's picture comes before us again: the scourging and mockery, the slow dying on the cross. It anticipated the fearful threefold experience of the victims of the Holocaust: that experience that one can be forsaken by all human beings, that one can even lose one's humanity, even can be abandoned by God.

So did Jesus' death have a meaning? My reply yet again is that a meaning can enter this outwardly meaningless, godforsaken dying only in the light of belief in the resurrection of Jesus to new life through and with God. Only on the basis of this faith is the crucified Jesus, exalted to God's eternal life, also the invitation to trust in a meaning even in apparently meaningless suffering and in this life to practise endurance and persistence to the end. So there is not the expectation of a happy ending on earth, as in the story which provides the framework to the book of Job, who ultimately can even beget seven sons and three daughters – to replace those whom he has lost. But quite radically there is the offer to affirm a meaning even in meaningless suffering (if need be, endured to the bitter end): a hidden meaning, which human beings cannot discover by themselves, but which can be given in the light of this one person, forsaken by God and man, and yet justified. For scripture, suffering and hope belong indissolubly together. This is hope in a God who despite everything will prove and establish himself not as an arbitrary God, capricious and impassible, but as a God of redeeming love.

So without suffering being trivialized, reinterpreted or glorified, or even just accepted stoically, impassively, without feeling, it can be recognized in the light of Jesus, the suffering servant of God, and confessed with almost desperate hope, in protest and prayer:
– that even when suffering is apparently meaningless, God is nevertheless hiddenly present;
– that while God does not preserve us *from* all suffering he does preserve us *in* all suffering;
– that wherever possible we should show solidarity in suffering and attempt to share in bearing it;
– indeed, that in this way we are not only enduring suffering but, where possible, fighting against it, less in individual matters than in the structures and conditions which cause suffering.

We must all decide for ourselves whether this is an answer which can be lived out, which helps us not to forget suffering but to come to terms with it. I have been moved and encouraged by the fact that even in Auschwitz, countless Jews and also some Christians believed in the God who despite all the terrors was nevertheless hiddenly present there, the God who not only suffered with them but also had mercy on them. They trusted and – this is often overlooked – prayed even in the hell of Auschwitz. Since then, many shattering testimonies have been collected which show that in the concentration camps not only was the Talmud recited secretly and festivals were observed, but that there were also prayers in trust to God even in the face of death.[40] Thus Rabbi Zvi Hirsch Meisel reports how on Rosh Hashanah, the Jewish New Year's Day, at risk of his life, he blew the shophar ('ram's horn') one last time at the request of 1400 young men condemned to death. When he left their block, a young man cried out: 'The Rebbe has strengthened our spirits by telling us that "even if a sharp sword rest on a man's throat, he should not despair of God's mercy". I say to you, we can hope that things will get better, but we must be prepared for them to get worse. For God's sake, let us not forget to cry out *shema yisrael* with devotion at the last moment.'[41] And so countless Jewish (and also some Christian) contemporaries in the concentration camps trusted that it made sense to accept their own suffering, to call on the hidden God, and where possible to support others. And because people prayed even in Auschwitz, while prayer after Auschwitz has not got any easier, at all events it certainly can never become meaningless.

To sum up: by this answer I have not provided a theoretical solution to the specific question why God 'did not intervene' and 'did not prevent it', because I cannot. But I have attempted to relativize it. It seems to me that in view of the tremendous negativity, in our own lives and in the history of the world, a middle way is offered to us theologically, Christians and Jews. On the one hand there is the godlessness of those who think to find in Auschwitz their strongest argument against God, and yet who nevertheless fail to explain anything. And on the other hand there is the belief in God of those who speculatively incorporate places like Auschwitz into trinitarian theology and elevate it into a dialectic of suffering within God, yet do not explain the ultimate cause of suffering either. This middle, modest way is the way of unshakeable (not irrational, but completely reasonable), boundless trust in God – despite everything: faith in a God who remains the light despite and in abysmal darkness. 'If God is for us, who is against us...? For I am sure that neither death, nor life, nor angels, nor principalities, nor things present, nor things to come, nor powers, nor height, nor depth, nor anything else in all creation will be able to separate us from the love of God in Jesus Christ our Lord' (Rom.8.31, 38f.) – thus the apostle Paul, who did not

IV

Descent into Hell – Resurrection – Ascension

Christian art lives by the figure of Christ. Yet for centuries in iconography people only dared to depict the suffering and death of Jesus Christ with symbols. This historical event was too offensive, too brutal. But what about his resurrection to eternal life? This wholly other event, transcending history, appeared too subtle, too spiritual. So here too, for example on sarcophagi, it was often only hinted at – with symbols and allegories: the cross with the Christ monogram and the garland of victory, the sun, the fish . . . Just as the prophet Jonah spent three days in the belly of the fish, so Jesus spent three days in the grave – a small reference to the symbolic significance of the three days between death and resurrection. But what about the event of the resurrection itself?

1. The image of the Risen One

The actual event of the raising of Christ is hardly depicted at all in images in the first millennium – with the exception, for example, of the illustration in the ninth-century Utrecht Psalter. Only from the twelfth century, the century of the Crusaders, does it become customary to depict Jesus' ascent from the tomb – victorious with the wound in his side and the banner with a cross. And the Renaissance artists of the fourteenth and fifteenth centuries were the first to venture to paint a risen figure hovering over the coffin – and mastered the technique for doing this. Here the master of the Umbrian school, Perugino, is far surpassed by his brilliant pupil Raffaello Sanzio with his 'Transfiguration' of Christ, which anticipates the resurrection.

But hardly any artist can match the power of artistic and religious expression of one who, though influenced both by the Italian Renaissance and Dutch painting, now depicted in a highly independent new way not only the crucified Christ but also the risen Christ: Matthias Grünewald, whom we are to remember again here. On the reverse of his Isenheim altar, on the other side of his crucified Christ, he also painted the risen Christ.

One can only guess what this picture-book leaf, opened on festivals, must have meant for the lepers in Isenheim covered in sores and blisters – as an image of the hope of a clean, whole body. What inner radiance there is in the colours which shine from it! The resurrection is depicted as a cosmic event, not against a golden background but against the black night sky with a few shining stars. In a powerful surge the risen Christ is soaring with arms uplifted, taking the white gravecloth with him, surrounded by an enormous radiance of light which turns into the colours of the rainbow and changes the cloth first into blue, then into violet, and in the centre into flaming red and yellow. What a symphony of colours! And that is the unique thing about this Easter picture: an unusual degree of spiritualization is achieved, and yet the body of the transfigured Christ remains clearly visible: the person of the risen Christ does not dissolve, but remains unmistakably a concrete figure, a definite person. The wound-marks on the alabastine body and the scarlet mouth recall that this is none other than the crucified Christ who – with the gesture of blessing and revelation – is entering the sphere of pure light. The face of the risen Christ, right in the centre, sunny, with an inner radiance, goes over into the blinding yellow of the aureole, which is like a sun. And though the outlines of the face are blurred by the shining light, with great tranquillity a pair of eyes look towards the beholder with gentle authority and reconciling grace. Truly, if an artist has ever succeeded in indicating in colour something that cannot really be painted, namely the *soma pneumatikon*, as the apostle Paul calls it, the 'pneumatic body', the spiritual body of the risen Christ, it is Grünewald.

'Beautiful, fine,' I hear contemporaries saying, 'but if you want to keep to the text of the Apostles' Creed, shouldn't Christ's descent into hell have been mentioned before the resurrection? And not only do some Christian painters know nothing of it, but even some Christian theologians keep quiet about it out of perplexity. Isn't this a somewhat curious article of faith?'

2. Descent into the underworld?

'*Descensus ad inferos*', a 'descent into the subterranean sphere', or *ad infera*, 'into the underworld', is indeed a remarkable article of faith which was also added to the church's creed only at a relatively late stage, in the second half of the fourth century (it was formulated by the Syrian Marcus of Arethusa at Sirmio in 359). And I concede that nowhere more clearly than in this article does it emerge that not all these articles of faith have the same significance and dignity. For – from a New Testament perspective – cross and resurrection are absolutely central: in the Gospels as in the apostolic epistles they stand at the centre. But what about the descent of Christ into the underworld? There is hardly any unambiguous piece of evidence for it in the New Testament, and even Augustine in his *Enchiridion*, his little handbook (written around 423), does not expound this article of faith because it was evidently not in the creed of his church. Today, almost two thousand years after the birth of Christ, no one would probably think of inserting this article into the Creed were it not already included in it.

The absence of an unambiguous biblical basis is doubtless the main reason for the ambiguity of this article of faith which has persisted down to the present day. It has again become evident in our day from the fact that the Catholic and Protestant churches in Germany, quite officially, without drawing much attention to it, have completely changed the translation of *descendit ad inferos* for the new ecumenical version of the Creed. Earlier it read 'he descended into hell', but now we have 'he descended into the realm of death'. Just a better translation? Not at all, but rather a tacit blurring of the meaning! For as a result of the reinterpretation an ambiguity comes into this article – though it had already been attached to this formula of faith from the Middle Ages.

For what is the destination of this *descensus*, this descent?

– Meaning 1: It is quite generally a 'realm of the dead', in Hebrew called Sheol and in Greek Hades, the place of all the departed, good and evil. That is how the *descensus* was understood in Christianity for more than a millennium, and the words 'hell' and 'descent into hell' were originally understood as it were neutrally as 'underworld' or 'realm of the dead'.

Meaning 2: It is a hell, the place of the non-blessed, Hebrew *gehenna*, Latin *infernum*, i.e. the place of those who are damned eternally. That is how the *descensus* has been understood since the Middle Ages. For now it was believed that immediately after death (depending on their good works or sins) the dying went into heaven ('paradise'), into purgatory, or into hell (*infernum*). In addition, in the Middle Ages people also assumed that there were two other subterranean areas, a 'pre-hell' or, with changing optimism, increasingly a 'pre-heaven', a place for the righteous of the Old Testament (*limbus patrum*) and a place for unbaptized children (*limbus puerorum*).

Since the tradition is so ambiguous, preachers today find themselves in an unenviable situation. Of course, they can choose freely, but this choice is between quite opposite interpretations of one and the same statement of faith. For it truly makes a difference whether a preacher has to present a congregation with 'hell', the definitive place of eternal damnation, or 'only' a realm of the dead, an intermediary place for everyone up to the Last Judgment. This is both a theological and a psychological difference. But so far no pope has ventured to decide, fallibly or infallibly, what this statement of faith ultimately means. Moreover the Reformers added a new psychological interpretation to the earlier explanations: 'descended into hell' – that means that Jesus even went through the torments of hell on the cross, by experiencing in death the wrath of God and the temptation of ultimate despair. But how do Luther and Calvin know that? There is certainly no scriptural evidence for it. The New Testament writings are not interested in Jesus' psychology. And what about the article on the 'descent'? Does that occur in scripture?

The only scriptural saying which has any relevance to Jesus' descent into the underworld, and which was associated with it from the time of Clement of Alexandria in the third century, is a passage from I Peter. Here is a mention of the dead Christ who went 'in the spirit' to preach to those spirits 'in prison' who were disobedient at the time of the flood (cf. I Peter 3.18-20). But even this text was interpreted in quite contradictory senses at different times by different authors. Today the most probable interpretation may be taken to be that this text, like similar texts from the apocryphal literature, especially the book of Enoch, speaks of the risen Christ transformed through the spirit who, like a new Enoch, proclaimed to the imprisoned angels (!) in the lower regions of heaven (where their 'prison' was) their definitive condemnation (!). In that case there would be no mention of a 'descent into hell' or into the realm of the dead in I Peter. So if spatial terms are retained, this is more like the first part of an ascension, through the lower regions of heaven to the upper. Furthermore, I Peter is a very late New Testament text and today can no longer be taken to have been written by an apostle like Peter. What then?

If we want clarification here, we must first of all openly concede that earlier pictures of the world can no longer be binding on the contemporary reader of the Bible: neither the picture of the world in the Hebrew Bible with its three-storey universe (heaven, earth, underworld) nor the Hellenistic picture of the world with an earth moving freely in space surrounded by planets, where the region above the moon is reserved for the gods and that under the moon for human spirits and the demonic powers who fight against human beings.

No wonder, then, that this article of faith, which was once so significant in the history of the church, has largely lost any existential significance for our contemporaries today. 'Descended into the realm of the dead', as the official translation now goes, is in any case better not understood along Reformation lines as a pychologizing insight into any conscious agony of Jesus, but rather as a symbolic expression in the spirit of the early church rather than the Reformation or the mediaeval church: here the risen Christ preached to the dead, above all the fathers of Israel, to take them with him into the heavenly kingdom, God's kingdom.

So, symbolically understood, the journey into the realm of the dead cannot be seen as a journey of suffering, as a last act of humiliation; nor is it a triumphal journey and a first act of exaltation. So even today the journey into the underworld can be understood as a symbol of the possibility of salvation for pre-Christian and thus non-Christian humanity: for the possibility of the salvation of the pious of the Old Testament who were not reached by the Christian proclamation, indeed for all the dead.

Such an interpretation is endorsed by the iconography of the Eastern church: in Byzantine art the descent of Jesus Christ into the realm of the dead has been depicted from around the seventh/ eighth centuries: however, it is important to note that it has clearly been portrayed as 'Anastasis', as 'resurrection'. Indeed such a portrayal, very widespread also in the West since the eleventh century, becomes the real portrayal of the resurrection in the Eastern Church: Christ gains the victory over the jaws of hell and fettered Satan. However, at the time of Grünewald, who in fact portrays the temptation of Anthony, the father of monasticism (in the monastery of the Antonites!), on a side panel of his altar in a mediaeval Western way, by fearful, grotesque, terrible demonic figures and (in an unconsciously Hellenistic way) by a battle of spirits in the air, among the greats almost only Dürer and Tintoretto still ventured to depict a descent by Jesus into hell, so that it is found increasingly rarely.

So, understood symbolically in connection with the resurrection, this article of faith need not cause any difficulties to contemporaries. However, it has to be conceded that it in particular shows how time-conditioned the Apostles' Creed is, even if, for the reasons that I have mentioned, increasing space is still given to it in the liturgy of the Eastern church.

Still, we can't ignore an interruption from a contemporary: 'If, then, the article of faith about the descent of Jesus Christ into hell is not of central importance, isn't that equally true of his ascent into heaven?' The answer is, 'No, it's not as simple as that.'

3. An ascension?

In contrast to Jesus' descent into hell, his ascension is mentioned in the New Testament itself: by the evangelist Luke. Luke's narrative is the basis for our article of faith. Which is also the problem: while Luke indeed mentions an ascension of Christ, he is the only one who does. We do not hear of it in either of the other two Synoptic Gospels (Mark and Matthew) or in John: nor is there a word either in Paul or in the Deutero-Paulines. In the earliest church of all there is no tradition of a visible ascension of Jesus before the eyes of the disciples.

Only Luke, the third evangelist, who in contrast to the other witnesses was *a priori* more interested than others in the proof of the bodily reality of the risen Christ and the eye-witness of the apostles, separates resurrection and ascension in time. That means that only Luke knows a separate ascension in Bethany which concludes the time of the appearances of Jesus on earth and emphatically opens the time of the world mission of the church, which lasts until Jesus' second coming. This is particularly clear in the Acts of the Apostles (written between 80 and 90), which Luke has as a sequel to his Gospel, perhaps written in the 70s. This idea of a separate ascension was then subsequently also inserted into the Gospel of Mark, at the end, at the same time taking up the story of the transportation of the prophet Elijah and the saying in the psalm about sitting at the right hand of the Father. But this so-called Marcan ending comes from the second century!

How is this ascension to be understood? Today one hardly needs to go into lengthy explanations of how talk of a 'journey' 'upwards' into 'heaven' – sometimes demonstrated in churches on the Feast of the Ascension by a statue of Christ being mechanically raised to the church roof – presupposes that ancient three-storey picture of the world which is no longer ours. As if Jesus in fact set out on a kind of space trip! It would be absurd to assert anything like that. But at that time, this idea which today would be thought impossible was not at all unusual. A journey into heaven is not only reported of Elijah and Enoch in the Hebrew Bible, but also of other great figures of antiquity like Heracles, Empedocles, Romulus, Alexander the Great and Apollonius of Tyana. Such ascensions were 'transportations' of great heroes in which they vanished from the earth; they were not real 'heavenly journeys', since neither the way to heaven nor the arrival in heaven is depicted. Indeed, usually the clouds soon cover those who are being transported – a sign of the simultaneous nearness and unapproachability of God.

From all this we can see that Luke's story of an ascension is not a Christian invention, is not an unprecedented, exorbitant 'miracle', but a model familiar to the hearers of the time. Luke had the transportation scheme at his disposal as a model and a narrative form. Presumably he himself shaped the traditional statements of the exaltation of Jesus to God into a transportation story, for which all the essential ingredients were available in the early stories about the empty tomb and the appearances. The only question is: why did he do this? There may have been two reasons for it.

First, Luke may have been primarily concerned to give help towards envisaging the intangible statements about exaltation: the risen Christ 'goes' to God, definitively enters God's reality. That means that the ascension of Jesus is not to be understood and celebrated as a second 'saving fact' after Easter, but as a specially emphasized aspect of the one Easter event. That is brought out by the fact that in the Gospel of Luke (and hence also in the conclusion to the Gospel of Mark), the ascension takes place on Easter Day itself. Only the Luke of the later Acts of the Apostles knows of a period of forty days between Easter and Ascension — evidently an allusion to the sacred biblical number forty: forty years of Israel in the wilderness, forty days of Elijah fasting, forty days of Jesus fasting. So the fact that the feast of the Ascension has clearly lost importance today in comparison to Easter is not to be judged simply in negative terms, but corresponds to the overall weighting of the New Testament itself.

Secondly, if we read the text attentively, it is striking that here the earlier 'imminent expectation' which was still widespread at the time, the early belief that Jesus would return in the lifetime of the first generation, is energetically corrected. As the disciples who remain behind are told, 'You men of Galilee, why do you stand looking up into heaven?' (Acts 1.11). Luke stresses a mission to the world instead of inactive waiting. It is not Jesus himself who has removed himself to heaven and left the disciples the task, but the Holy Spirit who will now come to equip the disciples for the time of mission which is now imminent, until finally — at the end of time — Jesus himself returns just as vividly. So in his ascension story Luke means to say that only those have understood Easter who do not stand gazing into heaven but go into the world and testify to Jesus.

But a contemporary now impatiently and rightly asks, 'Surely we now need an explanation of what this "Easter event" itself means? In the twentieth century isn't it quite nonsensical still to believe in a miracle like the story of the empty tomb?' Indeed the word Easter, which is connected with 'east' (dawn), was used for the feast of the resurrection only at a late stage. Now at a very early stage this was celebrated on the first day after the feast of the Passover in accordance with the report which already appears in Mark: 'On the first day of the week they (the women) came early to the tomb, when the sun was rising' (Mark 16.2). Does that mean that Christians must believe in the empty tomb?

4. Do we believe in the empty tomb?

We can very quickly get to the nub of the matter if we ask the simple question: who would suppose on finding an empty tomb that here someone had risen from the dead? Of itself, the mere fact of an empty tomb says nothing, for of course there could be many explanations for it. That is true today, and it was true then. And the evangelists themselves, probably to defend themselves against tendentious Jewish rumours, already report such explanations. Was the tomb empty? In that case the body must have been stolen, or there must have been some confusion, or the supposedly dead person must only apparently have died. Or even worse, in that case the story of a resurrection can only be a falsehood, put about by the disciples. Indeed, even now there are contemporaries who, contrary to all the plain statements of the authentic sources, believe in the theory that Jesus did not really die, and spread frivolous theories with sensational titles like 'Jesus the first new man'. Given the historical evidence, this is a nonsensical idea.

Let's be quite clear about it: the empty tomb as such is no proof of the truth of the resurrection of Jesus from the dead. That would quite clearly be begging the question: what is to be proved is presupposed. Of itself, the empty tomb only says 'He is not here' (Mark 16.6). And an explicit addition must already be made which is by no means a matter of course: 'He is risen' (Mark 16.6). But this can be said even without the preliminary sign of an empty tomb.

All this means that in itself, even according to the New Testament, the empty tomb did not lead to belief in the risen Christ (still in the Gospel of John, Peter does not believe because of the empty tomb; only the beloved disciple does, and this indicates that the recognition is brought about by God). Just as no one anywhere in the New Testament claims – as happens with Grünewald – to have been personally present at the resurrection or to know eye-witnesses of the event of the resurrection, so no one claims to have come to believe in the risen Christ through the empty tomb. Nowhere do the disciples appeal to the evidence of the empty tomb to strengthen the faith of the young Christian community or to refute and convince their opponents. So it is not surprising,

– that the earliest account of the appearances of Jesus (I Cor. 15.4) does not associate confession of the resurrection with the story of the empty tomb;

– that even Paul in all his letters nowhere mentions the 'empty tomb' or authoritative witnesses to the 'empty tomb' to support his message of the risen Christ;

– that finally the rest of the New Testament texts outside the Gospels are also silent about the empty tomb.

For us today that means that historically the tomb of Jesus may or may not have been open – belief in the new life of the risen Christ with God does not depend on the empty tomb. The Easter event is not determined by the empty tomb but at best illustrated by it. So the 'empty tomb' is not an article of faith or the ground or object of Easter faith, which means that it does not need to be mentioned in the Apostles' Creed either. Particularly those who wish to be faithful to the Bible need not believe on the basis of the empty tomb, still less believe 'in' the empty tomb. The Christian faith does not call on us to believe in the empty tomb; it calls us to an encounter with the living Christ himself: as we read in the Gospel, 'Why do you seek the living among the dead?' (Luke 24.5).

Furthermore, already in the New Testament the stories about the empty tomb differ markedly from one another: the soldiers guarding the tomb, who in Grünewald seem blinded by the radiance and are struck dumb to the ground, appear only in Matthew. Peter goes to the tomb only in Luke and John; the appearance to the women is only in Matthew and that to Mary of Magdala only in John. All this leads the majority of critical biblical exegetes to conclude that the stories about the tomb are legendary elaborations of the message of the resurrection in the style of Old Testament epiphany stories which were written down only many decades after Jesus' death.

For if we look closer, at the centre of the story of the tomb is not the empty tomb but the brief, confessional message of the resurrection (from the mouth of the angel), 'He is risen' (Mark 16.6). This is what we already find in the earliest document of the New Testament, the first letter to the Thessalonians, from 51/52, and time and again thereafter: Jesus, 'whom he (God) has raised from the dead' (I Thess.1.10). The story of the empty tomb is thus not to be seen as the recognition of a fact but as what was probably the early expression in narrative and growing legendary development of the prior message of the resurrection, a message which is contained in the proclamation of the angel(s).

So does it make sense to go on reading out these stories of the tomb on Easter Day? Certainly. What I have already said about the Christmas story also applies to these resurrection stories: a concrete story like that of the disciples on the road to Emmaus, a quite specific picture like that of Grünewald, can say more than a theoretical statement, a philosophical principle or a theological dogma. And the stories are all a sign which clarifies and confirms that all was not over with Jesus' death, that Jesus did not remain dead, and that the Risen Christ is none other than the executed Nazarene.

But here a contemporary trained in historical criticism will ask: 'As to the resurrection itself, mustn't we concede that belief in a resurrection of the dead appeared only very late in the Bible? Isn't the resurrection faith even fundamentally un-Jewish?'

5. Is resurrection from the dead un-Jewish?

The first thing to be said in reply is that belief in a life after death was an age-old Israelite conviction. But for centuries this life was imagined as a shadowy, joyless existence in an 'underworld' ('Sheol'). Only relatively late in Jewish history does belief in a new life after death appear: God raises the dead to a new life. The oldest, indeed the only undisputed passage in the Hebrew Bible which is evidence for this resurrection to a new, eternal life comes from the second-century BCE book of Daniel (around 165/4), i.e. a Jewish apocalyptic book. There is further evidence in the Greek Old Testament, especially in II Maccabees and the apocalyptic literature after Daniel. Here resurrection never – as, say, in the Greek world – means simply an immortality of the human 'soul' but, in accordance with the Jewish conception of the human being as a psychosomatic unity, a new life of the whole person with God.

So must Judaism and Christianity *a priori* recognize a difference here? Not at all, though the history of belief in the resurrection in Judaism is certainly changeable. 'Belief in the resurrection from the dead is an explicit dogma of classical Judaism, reaffirmed and elaborated by Moses Maimonides, treated by Hasdai Crescas as a "true belief" (rather than as a fundamental principle of Judaism), retracted to a more debatable level of a deduction by Joseph Albo, and all but lost as a central teaching ever since the close of the mediaeval discourse.' Thus Arthur A. Cohen, the biographer of Buber and professor at the University of Chicago, who continues: 'Nevertheless, despite its fall from the dogmatic eminence in which it, among other beliefs, was regarded as a *sine qua non* of rabbinic eschatological teaching, resurrection continues to be affirmed in the traditional liturgy. Introduced as the second blessing of the Eighteen Benedictions (the *Shemoneh Esreh*), repeated during the *Amidah* (lit. standing prayer), it asserts that God keeps faith with those who lie in the dust and will according to his mercy, raise the dead, restore them bodily and grant them eternal life.'[43]

So 'resurrection' by God is thoroughly Jewish. And not only is the content of the Christian faith Jewish: 'You are blessed, Yahweh, you bring the dead to life' (thus the wording of that second blessing, and the funeral liturgy is similar), but the form is Jewish also: 'God, who raised him from the dead' resembles the Jewish expressions of faith which are often used: 'God, who made heaven and earth' or, 'God who led you up out of Egypt'. Here already, however, it becomes clear that the subject of the resurrection is not Jesus, the one who has been killed, but God himself, who raises the dead, and to this degree it is less misleading to speak of 'raising' to avoid any suggestion that the Jesus is actively involved.

But, people may object, are not Jews and Christians divided by the fact that belief in God's power of resurrection is bound up with this one Jesus of Nazareth? Despite his hopeless end, Christians set their hopes on him; despite his shameful death, he was proclaimed Messiah. How can that be explained rationally?

6. Do we believe in the resurrection of the One?

Here first of all we have simply to note that according to all the testimonies, the reason given by the first disciples of Jesus, men and women, as the basis of their newly awakened faith, is the God of Israel and Jesus himself. In so doing they do not refer to any reflections on Jesus' overpowering personality, which 'could not die but lives' (as has long been sung of Lenin), nor even to any historical models (righteous sufferers and martyrs), but to evidently overwhelming appearances leading to public testimony which took place in the next days, weeks and months after Jesus' death, and for which Paul mentions a whole series of witnesses who are still alive (I Cor.15.5-8). These are experiences of the living Jesus which were granted to them unexpectedly. Certainly, our knowledge of spiritual experiences, visions, auditions, extensions of consciousness, ecstasies and 'mystical' experiences are still too limited for us to be able to explain what kind of reality ultimately underlies such stories. And certainly here the disciples resorted to patterns of interpretation that were already known at that time. But such experiences as people had cannot all be dismissed as hallucinations; nor, conversely, can they be explained in the supernaturalist scheme as an intervention of God from above or outside. Probably these will have been inward visionary events and not external reality. For 'subjective' psychological activity on the part of the disciples and 'objective' action by God are by no means exclusive: God can also work through the human psyche.

At all events, Jesus did not appear here publicly as the radiant victor with the banner of the cross in his hand, in the way in which he has been portrayed since the time of the Crusaders. These 'visions' or 'auditions', this 'seeing' and 'hearing', were not a natural, historical knowing but an event of trust which testified to it and in no way excluded doubt. These were experiences of faith which are best compared with the experience of the prophets of Israel at their call. Just as they also come to young men and women today, so that they recognize that they have been called, as the 'apostles of the Messiah Jesus', to preach the message and unconcernedly expose their lives to all kinds of dangers.

'But can't it be shown that there were also testimonies to other resurrections in antiquity?' Certainly, time and again there is mention above all of the story of an appearance of Apollonius of Tyana after his death, as reported by Philostratos. And doesn't that deprive the resurrection of Jesus of its special character? Here we should note the difference from the resurrection of Jesus. Did the story of this resurrection of Apollonius ever convince anyone to change their whole life, convince them that God had spoken and acted decisively through this one person? That is the special character of the resurrection of Jesus, not the form of history.

We do not know how far Jesus, who indeed may possibly have expected a dramatic eschatological turning point even during his lifetime, had himself prepared his disciples for such a dramatic event; the prophecies of death and resurrection as reported in the Gospels may only have been expressed in the form in which we have them at a later stage. The one thing that is certain is that the disciples, who had expected the kingdom of God in the near future, now saw this expectation fulfilled – in the resurrection of Jesus to new life. It was understood as the beginning of the eschatological redemption. That, too, was at least at the time a 'good Jewish' notion: not only the Jewish followers of Jesus but also many Jews in fact expected the resurrection of the dead at that time, since, as we heard, belief in the resurrection of the dead or at least of the righteous had emerged for the first time in the book of Daniel and the apocalyptic literature. However, what many Jews expected for all people in the future had now for the young Christian community already been anticipated, on the basis of their Easter experiences, in this one person: the resurrection of Jesus was the beginning of the general resurrection of the dead, the beginning of the end-time with a respite until the appearance of the 'Son of man' who was to be expected (according to Dan.7.13). That appeared well founded in the Jewish world of faith of the time.

The followers of the crucified Jesus of Nazareth stand in this apocalyptic tradition. They never presented the resurrection of Jesus as the miracle of raising a dead person to this life, of a kind already reported in three cases in the Hebrew Bible, but always as a resurrection of the dead to heavenly, definitively changed life. It was the steadfast conviction of this first Christian community that this crucified one had not fallen into nothing, but from provisional, transitory, impermanent reality had entered into the true, eternal life of God. God did not leave this righteous one in the lurch; he secured justice for him through death, he 'justified' him, indeed exalted him to be 'Son'.

For where is the one who has been raised from death now? We have already heard the answer to what was then a tremendously urgent question. The first Christians gave it above all in words from a psalm which have now found their way into the Apostles' Creed. He 'is seated at the right hand of the Father'. In fact no sentence in the Hebrew Bible is quoted or alluded to in the New Testament more often than Psalm 110.1: 'The Lord said to my Lord, "Sit at my right hand!" ' This does not express a 'community of being' but – and this was the maximum that a Jew could say as a monotheist – a 'throne community' of the risen Jesus with God his Father, on the 'throne of glory', the 'throne' of God himself.[44] And the image of the throne, taken from the world of royal imagery, is of course to be understood as a symbol of rule, so that the kingdom of God and the messianic kingdom in fact become identical. 'Jesus is the Lord' (in Hebrew the 'Maran', in Greek the 'Kyrios'): this is the oldest confession of faith in the Chrsitian community – directed against all the other rulers of this world.

As we saw, the message of the resurrection of the crucified Christ has not been handed down without time-conditioned imagery and legendary elaborations, without extensions and developments conditioned by the situation. And yet fundamentally it culminates in something simple, which from the beginning is expressed unambiguously by all the witnesses through all the discrepancies, indeed contradictions, of the tradition: the crucified one is alive and rules for ever with God – as an obligation and a hope for us! Jewish Christians and later also Gentile Christians from the New Testament communities were borne up, indeed fascinated and enthused, by the certainty that this dead man had not remained dead but was alive, and that anyone who held to him and followed him would live also. Death is not God's last word about human beings. The new, eternal life of the one is a challenge and a real hope for all.

In this way it has become clear that, from the beginning, the fact that all was not over at Jesus' death, that he himself did not remain dead, but entered into God's eternal life, was not a proven historical fact, but always a conviction of faith. And this faith does not call for the idea of a 'supernatural' intervention by a *Deus ex machina*, contravening all the laws of nature. This faith rests on the conviction of a 'natural' dying and being received into the real, true, divine reality, understood as a final human state of human beings without any suffering. Just as Jesus' dying cry 'My God, my God, why have you forsaken me?' (Mark 15.34) is already turned into a positive statement in Luke's Gospel with the saying from a psalm, 'Father, into your hands I commend my spirit' (Ps.31.6; Luke 23.46), and then in John with 'It is fulfilled' (19.3).

But there might be an objection: 'So don't you take literally the statement of faith about God who brings the dead to life? Don't Christians have to believe in the revival of a dead person, in a physical resurrection in the physiological sense?' This question of contemporaries is quite justified, so I must immediately explain:

7. What 'resurrection' does and does not mean

It has already become clear that the earliest, brief testimonies of the New Testament do not understand Jesus' resurrection as a revival to earthly life – and therefore as an analogy to those Old Testament resuscitations by prophets. Rather, against the horizon of Jewish apocalyptic expectation, here is clearly the exaltation of this executed and buried Nazarene through God to God, to a God whom he himself called 'Abba', 'Father'.

So what is meant by 'resurrection'? I can now give a summary answer to the question:

– Resurrection does not mean a return to life in this space and time. Death is not reversed (there is no revival of a corpse), but definitively overcome: entry into a wholly other, incorruptible, eternal, 'heavenly' life. Resurrection is not a 'public fact'.

– Resurrection does not mean a continuation of this life in space and time. Even talk of 'after' death is misleading; eternity is not defined by a temporal before and after. Rather, it means a new life which bursts the dimensions of space and time, new life in God's invisible, incomprehensible sphere, symbolically called 'heaven'.

– Positively, resurrection means that Jesus did not die into nothing, but in death and from death died into that ineffable and incomprehensible last and first reality, was accepted by that most real reality, which we denote by the name God. Where human beings reach their eschaton, the ultimate point of their lives, what awaits them there? Not nothingness, but that All which is God. The believer now knows that death is a transition to God, is an entry into God's hiddenness, into that sphere which transcends all our notions, which no human eye has ever seen and which is thus removed from our grasp, understanding, reflection and imagination! If that word mystery, so misused in theology, is appropriate anywhere, then because here it relates directly to God's ownmost sphere, it is appropriate in the resurrection to new life.

In other words, the faith of the disciples is not just a historical fact which can be grasped by historical means – as is also the case with the death of Jesus: resurrection by God to eternal life is not a historical event, an event which can be envisaged and imagined, even a biological event, but it is nevertheless a real event in the divine sphere. What does that mean? What does 'live' mean here? Simply a look at Grünewald's picture of the resurrection warns us that the risen Christ is not another, purely heavenly being, but that man Jesus of Nazareth who was crucified, who is still corporeal and yet is spiritualized. And even through the resurrection this man does not become an indeterminate fluid, fused with God and the universe, but even in the life of God remains this particular, irreplaceable one who he was – though without the spatial and temporal limitations of his earthly form. Hence in Grünewald the transition of the face into pure light. According to the biblical witnesses, death and resurrection do not abolish the identity of the person but preserve it in an unimaginable, changed form, in a completely different dimension.

What is the consequence? For us today, with our education in science, it has to be said quite plainly that God does not need the bodily remannts of the earthly existence of Jesus for the identity of the person to be preserved. This is resurrection to a completely different form of existence. It might perhaps be compared with that of a butterfly, which flies out of the dead caterpillar. Just as the same living being strips off the old form of existence (the caterpillar) and takes on an unimaginably new, utterly free, light, airy new form of existence (the butterfly), so we may imagine the event of the transformation of our self by God. This is an image. We are not obliged to hold any kind of physiological ideas of resurrection.

But in that case, what is resurrection bound to? Not to the substratum or the elements of this particular body, which *a priori* change constantly, but to the identity of the one irreplaceable person. The corporeality of the resurrection does not demand – either then or now – that a dead body should be brought to life. For God raises in a new form, one which can no longer be imagined; as Paul paradoxically puts it, as a *soma pneumatikon*, as a 'pneumatic body', in 'spiritual corporeality'. By this remark, which is indeed paradoxical, Paul wanted to convey two things at the same time: continuity – since 'corporeality' stands for the identity of the former person, who is not simply dissolved, as though his or her previous history, experienced and suffered, had become irrelevant. And at the same time discontinuity – for 'spirituality' does not simply stand for a continuation or revival of the old body, but for the new dimension, the infinite dimension, which comes into effect, changing all that is finite after death.

'But is the idea of a single life to be taken over quite so uncritically?', at least a contemporary influenced by Indian spirituality might ask. 'Aren't there quite different ideas in other religions, e.g. Indian religions, which contrast with the Jewish-Christian-Islamic conviction and provide a major alternative? Don't human beings have several lives, so that we can improve step by step until we enter the last, supreme reality, Nirvana, or whatever it may be called? So why not have belief in rebirth into this life, reincarnation or transmigration, instead of resurrection?'

8. Just one life or several?

There are many reasons why for centuries a large proportion of humankind has believed in reincarnation or rebirth. In all religions of Indian origin – among Hindus, Buddhists and Jainas – reincarnation is a dogma which is never proved, but accepted *a priori*. This is not the case, however, in the third religious river system: the Chinese generally reject reincarnation, as do the prophetic religions of the first river system: Judaism, Christianity and Islam. But it also appears among the ancient Greeks, among the Pythagoreans (perhaps under Indian influence), in Plato and the Neo-Platonists, and in Virgil. Indeed it has key witnesses even in German classicism and romanticism, although Kant, Lessing, Lavater, Herder, Goethe and Schopenhauer may perhaps have accepted the doctrine of reincarnation only for a time.

I need not go here into Nietzsche's doctrine of the eternal return of the same – I have described it and discussed it thoroughly elsewhere; it is an age-old, but highly ambivalent, myth of humankind with which Nietzsche wanted to avert the threat of nihilism produced by atheism and to stabilize himself – but without success. Nor do I want to describe why I quite personally, for all my joy in life, don't feel the slightest inclination after death to return to life on this earth, in whatever form. I simply want to indicate briefly that since there are important arguments for believing in a rebirth into this life, it also makes sense to believe in a resurrection to definitive, eternal life.

My presupposition here is that just as no one, strictly speaking, has proved the reality of resurrection to a new and eternal life, so too no one has proved the fact of a repeated life on earth. Of course there are extended accounts of people who can recall their former life. But it has not been possible to provide convincing verification of any of these reports of a recollection of a (!) former life – most originally by children and coming from lands in which there is belief in reincarnation – and the same is true of the narrative of the Buddha's recollection of 100,000 lives that he lived previously, which was written down so many centuries after his death and which is evidently legendary. Therefore even many anthroposophists regard the doctrine of reincarnation less as a theory which has been scientifically proved than as an unprovable conviction of faith. Nor are there any scientifically undisputed, generally acknowledged facts for belief in reincarnation from the sphere of parapsychology – not to mention spiritism and theosophy. However, it is certain that the arguments for reincarnation – both retrospective, looking back, and prospective, forward-looking – have no less weight. Most of them centre on the religious and philosophical question of a moral order of the world, i.e. the tormenting question of justice in a world in which human destinies are so terrifyingly different and seem to be distributed unfairly. Therefore:

Question 1, retrospective: doesn't a truly moral ordering of the world necessarily presuppose the idea of a life before the present life? Can the inequalities of opportunity among human beings, the confusing difference of moral dispositions and individual fates, be explained satisfactorily unless one assumes that human beings have themselves caused their present fate by their good and evil deeds in earlier life on earth? Wouldn't this explain why things so often go badly with the good (because of former guilt) and well with the evil (because of former good deeds). So a doctrine of rebirth seems to have much to be said for itself, as it is based on 'Karma' (Sanskrit 'action', 'work'), i.e. on the 'effect' of good and evil actions which determine each human fate in present life and in future births.

But I have a few questions to ask in return:
– Can my present destiny really be satisfactorily explained by an earlier destiny? This earlier destiny would itself in turn have to be explained by a yet earlier one and this in turn by one even earlier, resulting in a chain of rebirths to infinity – but this is something that Hindus and Jainas do not accept. However, the further back the causal chain is pursued, the more impersonal my fate becomes! Can it really help me if my present life is ultimately to be explained from grey times in the past to which I have no kind of relationship?
– But presupposing that a beginning is established at God's creation: what are we to think of this primal beginning which necessitates a second life and is meant not to burden the creator with this creature which evidently went wrong at the first creation?
– Wouldn't an explanation of our moral dispositions by rebirth fall into an unhistorical individualism which largely overlooks what does not come to us specifically from a postulated former

life but is communicated through biological genes, the formation of our conscious and unconscious in early childhood, through our primary relationships to persons and finally through the whole social situation? Is the problem of theodicy then really solved by reincarnation?

– If in general a radical forgetting of any former life has to be assumed, then is personal identity preserved, since very little is recalled of a self? And what does it help me to know that I have already lived, if I have utterly forgotten this life?

– Doesn't the doctrine of reincarnation finally do away completely with respect for the mystery of the individual whose fate (why born in this particular way, here and now, and not at another place and in another time?) cannot ultimately be deciphered by human beings? Doesn't it also do away with respect for the mystery of the Godhead, who is not entrusted with a just and merciful assignment and assessment of fate and suffering? Isn't this the harsh causal law of Karma instead of the love of God, which graciously comprehends good and evil deeds in justice and mercy?

Question 2, prospective: Doesn't a truly moral world order necessarily presuppose the idea of a life after this life? For how is the expiatory compensation for actions, which so many people rightly expect, to come about (one thinks of the murderers and their victims), and how is the necessary ethical perfection to develop in human life unless the opportunity is given of a further life? So reincarnation is an appropriate retribution for all works, good and evil, and also serves for the moral cleanisng of human beings!

But here, too, a few questions need to be asked in return:

– Doesn't the demand for expiatory compensation in another historical life fail to recognize the seriousness of history, which lies in its unique and unrepeatable character, so that anything that is once neglected can never return?

– Aren't there disruptions in the world order which can never be reversed again by any human action, which cannot be recompensed but only forgiven? Indeed, isn't it part of the human (or perhaps Christian) notion of guilt that while perhaps guilt cannot be forgotten it can be 'forgiven', instead of having to be fully expiated in accordance with an iron, superhuman law? So why not the gracious God instead of the inexorable causal law of Karma?

But some contemporaries will object: 'Then why has the doctrine of reincarnation found so many new adherents in our days?' This seems to me not least to be connected with two deficiencies in traditional Christian doctrine:

1. Nowadays the traditional belief in a 'purgatory', as it were a second life after our earthly life which is to blot out all guilt before a person can enter into a third, eternal life, has largely disappeared even in Catholicism. But there has been hardly any thought that dying and entering into eternity cannot simply be one and the same thing for the murderers and their victims, if at least at the end there is to be any justice.

2. Eternal life in a supra-terrestrial 'heaven', 'eternity', is traditionally presented by Christianity in such a boring, static way, so remote from any dynamic and future, indeed individual, development, that it is no surprise that in a famous sketch by Ludwig Thoma the Munich man condemned to sing Hallelujah for ever on a heavenly cloud longs for a life on this earth and a return to his beloved Hofbräuhaus. If the doctrine of reincarnation has an element of truth in it, it is that eternal life is real life, and does not exclude but includes unsuspected further developments, not in the sphere of finitude, but in infinity. We must return to the questions of heaven and hell concealed in these problems.

Be that as it may, the Jewish-Christian-Islamic tradition offers an alternative solution to the doctrine of reincarnation, which is confirmed by the Far-Eastern, Chinese tradition that also has an influence in Korea, Japan and Vietnam: human beings do not travel to purification, cleansing, liberation, perfection through several earthly existences. Human destiny is decided in this earthly life, and after this life by an irrevocable act of a gracious God.

'But are you sure?' someone will ask me. 'Most people have made their choice on this question anyway, or have grown into it from earliest childhood.' Yes, I'm aware of that. But many people keep doubting again, especially in limit-situations. Here, as in the case of belief in God itself, it is never a matter of rational decisions but of decisions of the whole person, who is more than just reason and who nevertheless may not be irrational. And here one thing seems to me to be particularly important. In the end, belief in the resurrection is not some curiosity or speciality of faith, but no more and no less than a radicalized faith in God.

9. Radicalization of belief in the God of Israel

In fact everyone, whether Jew, Christian, Muslim, believer or non-believer, is here faced with the last great alternative in their lives: for human beings, is dying dying into nothingness or into an ultimate reality? Do human beings die into a ultimate meaninglessness or into God's most real reality? But is this 'dying into God' so clear a matter?

No, it is not. Dying into God is anything but a matter of course. It is not a natural development, a desideratum of human nature to be fulfilled unconditionally. Death and resurrection must be distinguished, not necessarily in time but in content. Death is a human affair; the new life can only be God's affair or, more precisely, God's gift, God's grace. Human beings are taken up, called, brought home by God's Spirit into God's incomprehensible, all-embracing ultimate reality, and thus ultimately accepted and saved. This happens in death, or better from death, as a separate event, grounded in God's action and faithfulness. As at the first creation at the beginning, so at the end there is a hidden, unimaginable, new creative act of the one who calls into being that which is not. And therefore it is a real event, as real as God is utterly real for those who believe in him – and not a supernatural 'intervention', contrary to the laws of nature.

So whether understood in Jewish or Christian terms, belief in the resurrection is not an addition to belief in God but a radicalization of belief in God. It is a belief in God who does not stop half-way but continues consistently right to the end. It is a faith in which, without strictly rational proofs, but in completely reasonable trust, human beings rely on the fact that the God of the beginning is also the God of the end; that just as he is the creator of the world and human beings, so too he is their perfecter.

Belief in the resurrection can and should change our life here and now: unconditional commitment to this one life here and now should and can be motivated and strengthened by an ultimate sense of living and dying, as is attested by countless examples. And yet belief in the resurrection is to be interpreted not just as an existential internalization or social change, but as a radicalization of belief in the creator God. Resurrection means the real overcoming of death by God, to whom believers entrust all things, including the last things, and even the overcoming of death. It is the end that is a new beginning! So those who begin their creed with belief in 'God the almighty creator' may also confidently end it with belief in the 'eternal life' which is God himself. Becuse God is the Alpha, he is also the Omega. That means that the almighty creator who calls into being from nothingness may also call from death to life.

What reason do Christians in particular have for this belief? Here a quite basic answer must be given: nothing but the conviction that has come to them that by the resurrection God himself has justified the crucified Christ, the innocent man who was executed. Although an obvious failure among human beings, he had been justified before God. God had identified his own self with this godforsaken one. God took the side of the one who had completely relied on him, who had given his life for God's cause and the human cause. God acknowledged him, and not the hierarchy of Jerusalem which had put him on trial, or the Roman military power which had condemned him and executed him. God said 'yes' to his proclamation, his conduct, his fate.

That means something like a 'revaluation of all values', a revaluation above all, as we have heard, of suffering. And as far as Jesus himself is concerned, the Christian messianic faith reversed the polarity of the traditional Jewish title of Messiah and the traditional messianic expectation. 'Messiah', this title of the one who was to bear authority and bring salvation in the end-time, could have many meanings. Understood in the broadest political and Jewish-nationalistic sense, and later also often fused with the apocalyptic understanding of the Son of Man, 'Messiah of God' meant the mighty warrior hero of the end-time and the royal liberator of the people. But as a result of the fate of Jesus, the title Messiah was now given a completely new interpretation. Now it denoted a non-violent, defenceless, misunderstood, persecuted, betrayed and finally even suffering and dying Messiah, already prefigured for early Christianity in the Servant Songs of the book of Isaiah. To normal Jewish understanding this must have sounded as scandalous as the corresponding title put on the cross at the passion, 'King of the Jews'. In this completely transformed sense, even after the New Testament the title Messiah, in Greek Christ, has remained for Christianity down to the present day the most frequent honorific title for Jesus of Nazareth; indeed, it is used as a proper name. But there is a question which cannot be avoided: 'Down to the present day, doesn't the understanding between Christians and Jews come to grief on this view of Messiahship?' Indeed, here we have a most profound decision of faith.

10. A decision of faith

Though there may be a historical dispute over the question of the preaching, actions and self-understanding of Jesus, the profile of Jesus' Jewishness and the belief of the earliest Jewish-Christian community, this question still remains in the sphere of historical research, which deals in categories of more or less, more probable or less probable. However, at this point another dimension comes into play: the real but not historically controllable dimension of God himself. At this point Christians must contribute their own reasonable trust, their decision of faith, which they can never force on anyone else. Here there is no more or less, more probable or less probable, but only a yes or no. This is a decision of faith to which there is no compulsion, but a manifold invitation: a decision that the one God, the God of creation and the exodus, the God of the prophets and the wise men of Israel, has not just spoken and acted through the patriarchs, the prophets and the wise men, but also finally and definitively through the prophet from Nazareth – indeed has revealed himself through him in a unique way: through him, God's 'Messiah', 'Christ', 'Lord' and 'Son'.

Despite everything – and here Jews and Christians again agree in principle – the resurrection of the One is still not the consummation of the whole. Here Christians should not contradict Jews, who have long professed the resurrection: even after Jesus, the Christ, the world has not been changed; its distress is too great. Even for Christians, the final redemption and consummation is still to come: the 'parousia' has not yet taken place – either for Jews or for Christians. God's kingdom will first come comprehensively and in an all-determining way. So Jesus' petition 'Thy kingdom come' in the 'Our Father' can stand, as can the petition to Jesus, 'Marana-tha', 'Lord, come', come soon!

On the other hand, it was already the conviction of those Jews who followed Jesus that everything must not be expected only from that coming kingdom. Why? Because in Jesus himself, his liberating words and healing actions, and above all through his resurrection from the dead, the power of the coming kingdom has now already dawned, the great sign has been set for the coming redemption of the world; the beginning of redemption, an initial redemption, has already taken place. Though Jesus' first followers may even have been deceived over the time of the ultimate consummation, this fact of a 'present eschatology' which was already being fulfilled now also opens up a perspective on the future whose consummation Jews and Christians together await. For Christians, however, the one who has come is someone who does not just proclaim the kingdom of God but in his words and deeds is at the same time its guarantee. For Christians he is the Messiah, the Christ – the decisive reason why the Jews who followed Jesus at that time could be called 'Christians' in Greek.

So may the resurrection of Jesus be understood triumphalistically from the Christian side as a victory over Judaism? Unfortunately this has happened all too often. On the Christian side, everything possible has been grounded in belief in the resurrection of Jesus: that Judaism has been superseded, and with it the triumphalism of the church over the Jewish people. This first opened the way to anti-Judaism – specifically with reference to the resurrection of the crucified Jew from Nazareth.

On this it has to be said that the resurrection of Jesus is certainly an indispensable basic substance of Christian faith. But it must not be understood in an anti-Jewish, fundamentalist way. Paul himself reminds all Christian triumphalists in Corinth that the Risen Christ is and remains the Crucified Christ, so that no one has any reason for triumphalism and boasting here. If the resurrection is understood in accordance with scripture, it may not in any way be seen as a message against the Jews. It is not an un-Jewish truth which is meant to smash people down, but a truth deriving from Judaism which is simply meant to give hope. It does not supersede a Jewish truth, but confirms it. The risen Lord is an invitation to a great decision against death for life, which each person has to make in his or her own way.

V

Holy Spirit: Church, Communion of Saints and Forgiveness of Sins

It wasn't easy to speak to contemporaries of God, and even less so to speak of God's Son. But how is one to speak of God's Holy Spirit, who cannot be grasped or depicted, and certainly cannot be painted?

1. Spiritualized painting

Now in the history of Western art there is one painter to whom more than anyone else a drive towards spiritualizing is attributed. Many of his pictures have flashes of ecstatic unrest. The space which he paints is often more hinted at symbolically than real space; verticals, upwards-striving movement, predominate; his figures seem artificially stretched, unnaturally extended; the contrast of light and shade is highly dramatic; the outlines flicker. And if there is beauty, then here it is largely dematerialized – apart from the expressive eyes of many of his figures.

This painter comes from a background of Greek, Byzantine art, but in Venice and Rome he took over from the great masters Titian, Bassano and Tintoretto the achievements of the Renaissance and Mannerism. And he combined all this with the mystical popular religion of Spain – himself no Spaniard, yet more Spanish than the Spaniards. He is Domenikos Theotokopoulos from Crete, called El Greco (1541-1614), and was not only a painter but also a sculptor, architect and art theoretician.

In his last creative period this very cultivated artist, almost seventy years old and increasingly helped in his work by his son, ventured a portrayal which is found far more rarely in Western painting than subjects like Christmas, Good Friday or Easter: a picture of Pentecost, the feast of the outpouring of the Holy Spirit. In this picture, which strives vertically upwards – it is now in the Prado in Madrid – one can see in dematerialized scenery against a grey-green background a group of people seized by the Spirit, consisting of two women and a dozen men. Passionate excitement, to be read from their faces and gestures, has seized them: some are throwing their hands in the air; others are craning their necks; yet others are looking upwards in a mystic trance. Above are ten figures, almost as in a Greek-Byzantine picture, all on the same level, and below them are figures set at an angle, leaning back in surprise. Their garments, in markedly restrained colours – green, blue, yellow, red and ochre – are illuminated from above. And over each of the figures hovers a bright little tongue of fire, which makes them even more emphatic, moved, entranced. It is a highly dramatic picture of almost expressionist boldness, yet it is concentrated, de-reified, spiritualized.

And what of the spirit itself, the Holy Spirit? This appears high up in a divine splendour of light, which illuminates the darkness of space, depicted by that symbol which from the baptism of Jesus was used at a very early stage for portrayals of Pentecost: the symbol of the dove. It continued to be dominant down to the early Middle Ages and then was taken up again after the sixteenth/ seventeenth centuries, precisely at the time of El Greco.

'But isn't there constant mention in theology – following some statements in the Gospel of John – of the Holy Spirit as a person (the "Comforter")? And so doesn't he often appear, at least in mediaeval art, directly in human form?'

Yes, indeed, in mediaeval art the Spirit is often depicted along with God and his Son as a third of three equal human forms – as it were three angels or three Gods. Or precisely the opposite: from the thirteenth century to the Italian Renaissance the Trinity of Father, Son and Spirit was often even portrayed as a single figure with three heads or three faces (*trikephalos*) – a Godhead in three modalities. But aren't both tritheism and modalism equally unacceptable for contemporaries today?

However, we should listen and wonder: both portrayals were banned by the popes: Urban VIII banned these all-too-human images of the Trinity as early as 1628, and since the enlightened Benedict XIV (1745) the Holy Spirit may be depicted only in the form of a dove, a decision which in our century was again stressed in 1928 by the Holy Office, the Roman Inquisition, now called the Congregation of Faith. This raises the basic question:

2. What does Holy Spirit mean?

How did people in the ancient biblical period imagine the 'spirit' and God's invisible activity? Tangible yet intangible, invisible yet powerful, as important to life as the air that we breathe, laden with energy like the wind, the storm – that is the Spirit. All languages know a word for it, and the way in which it is given different genders shows that the Spirit cannot be determined so easily: *spiritus* in Latin is masculine (as is *Geist* in German); *ruach* in Hebrew is feminine; and the Greek has the neuter *pneuma*.

So spirit is at any rate something quite different from a human person. According to the beginning of the creation story the *ruach* is that 'breath' or 'storm' of God which moves over the waters. According to the New Testament the *pneuma*, too, is contrasted with the 'flesh', with created transitory reality, and is the living power and force which emanates from God. So spirit is that invisible power and force of God which can have a creative or indeed a destructive effect, for life or for judgment, which works in both creation and in history, in Israel as later also in the Christian communities. According to the biblical writings this power can come upon people powerfully or gently, and bring ecstasy to individuals or to groups, like the group in El Greco's picture. The spirit works in the great men and women, in Moses and the 'judges' of Israel, in warriors, singers and kings, in prophets and prophetesses and – as in our picture – in apostles and disciples. The centre of the picture is clearly marked by Mary the mother of Jesus in red, inclining towards the young Mary of Magdala.

But how far is this spirit the *Holy* Spirit? The Spirit is 'Holy' in so far as it is distinguished from the unholy spirit of human beings and their world, and has to be seen as the Spirit of the one holy God himself. The Holy Spirit is God's Spirit. Also in the New Testament the Holy Spirit is not – as it is often in the history of religion – some magical, substantial, mysterious-supernatural fluid of a dynamic nature (no spiritual 'something'), nor is it a magical being of an animistic kind (no spiritual being or ghost). In the New Testament, too, the Holy Spirit is none other than God! God in so far as God is near to human beings and the world, indeed becomes an inner force as the power which grasps but cannot be grasped, the force which creates life but also brings judgment, the grace which gives, but is under no one's control.

'However,' someone might interrupt, 'doesn't the very symbol of the dove (originally the messenger bird of the ancient Eastern goddess of love), which has ultimately again displaced the depiction of the Holy Spirit in human form, have anthropomorphic associations?' The answer is that in any case, this symbol for the motherly-feminine, life-giving dimension, the symbol for love and peace, which possibly found its way into the story of Jesus' baptism from the early Jewish wisdom tradition (Philo),[45] emphasizes the feminine dimension in God which indeed is as important as the masculine, since (as must be stressed yet again) the differentiation of the sexes is included and at the same time transcended in God himself. But it has to be conceded that most misunderstandings about the Holy Spirit stem from the way in which it has been separated from God and made independent like a mythological form of God. Here the Council of Constantinople of 381 in particular, that council to which we owe the expansion of the originally christological creed of the Council of Nicaea in 325 to the Holy Spirit, explicitly stresses that the Spirit is of one substance with Father and Son.

So in no way may the Holy Spirit be understood as a third element, as a thing between God and human beings. No, Spirit means the personal nearness of God to human beings, as little to be separated from God as the sun's rays are to be separated from the sun itself. So if it is asked how the invisible, intangible God is near, present to believing human beings, the community of faith, then the unanimous answer of the New Testament is: God is near to us human beings in the Spirit; God is present in the Spirit, through the Spirit, indeed as Spirit. And if it is asked how the Jesus Christ who is taken up to God and exalted is near to believers and the community of faith, then according to Paul the answer is that Jesus has become a 'life-giving Spirit' (I Cor.15.45). Indeed,

'The Lord (i.e. the Kyrios, Jesus, the exalted one) is the Spirit' (II Cor.3.17). That means that God's Spirit is now at the same time the Spirit of the one exalted to God, so that the Lord exalted to God is now in the mode of existence and activity of the Spirit. Therefore he may be present through the Spirit, in the Spirit, as Spirit. The encounter of God, Kyrios and Spirit with the believer is really one and the same encounter. However, it should be noted that God and God's Christ are not just present through the subjective recollection of human beings or through faith. Rather, they are present through the spiritual reality, presence, efficacy of God and Jesus Christ himself as they encounter human beings.

'But from heaven back to earth and back to Pentecost again. Is Pentecost a historical event?' This sceptical question of the contemporary is justified. Is it perhaps also already reflected in the face of the painter El Greco, who painted himself into his own picture of Pentecost – so to speak as the thirteenth of the apostles. He is not drawn upwards in rapture but coolly looks the viewer straight in the face. What might he be thinking?

3. Pentecost – a historical event?

Jesus proclaimed the kingdom of God; the church came! This often-quoted *bon mot* seems sharp, but has some truth to it: in his lifetime Jesus did not found what is now called the 'church', a major religious organization. It says much for the authenticity of the tradition, which was evidently not painted over by the early church, that the Gospels do not know of any sayings of Jesus addressed to the public which programmatically call for the founding of a community and announce the organization of a fellowship of the elect. Even the parables of the fishing net and the leaven, the parables of seed and growth, do not point to the founding of a church, but describe the growth of the future kingdom of God. And even after the founding of a church, this kingdom of God is not identical with that church. Neither the followers of Jesus nor the disciples especially called to follow him, or the Twelve, were singled out by Jesus from Israel as the 'new people of God' or 'church' and contrasted with Israel, the people of God. This insight must be fundamental to present-day Jewish-Christian dialogue: Jesus addressed all Israel and did not want any substitution of the old people of God with a new one. What does that mean, then? Does a church in the name of Jesus have any theological legitimation at all?

There is no disputing the fact that only after Jesus' death and resurrection does earliest Christianity speak of an 'assembly', Hebrew *qahal*, Greek *ekklesia*, Latin *ecclesia*. The 'church' in the sense of a special community distinct from Israel is clearly a post-Easter entity. Here the *ekklesia* comes into being under the impact of the Spirit of the risen 'Kyrios' or 'Lord', and it is no coincidence that the English word 'church' is ultimately derived from the Greek 'Kyrios'. So the *ekklesia* doesn't come into being through a formal act of institution and foundation. The *ekklesia* is there only by a constantly new specific event of meeting, assembly, and especially liturgical assembly, in the Spirit of Christ. That is the theological legitimation of the church. This tangible assembly is the present manifestation, representation, indeed realization of the community. Conversely, the community is the abiding vehicle of the event of the assembly which takes place anew time and again. So what is decisive for the church is not an 'act of founding' which can be demonstrated historically; rather, what is decisive is the particular 'event' church, which always becomes reality when people meet together, pray together, celebrate together, act together – wherever, however and whenever – as disciples of Christ and in memory of him.

This in particular can be made clear from the overpainted legend of Pentecost, though at Pentecost there is no act of founding the church, authenticated by a notary; what takes place is the church as 'event', an event under the influence of the Spirit of God. First of all, however, it must be seen that neither Paul nor Mark nor Matthew knows anything of a special Christian 'Pentecost'. Indeed, for an evangelist like John, Easter and Pentecost, resurrection and the giving of the Spirit, even expressly coincide.

Again we know only from Luke's relatively late Acts of the Apostles of the existence of an event of the sending of the Spirit separate from Easter, on a day which for Jews was harvest festival ('*Pentekoste*' is Greek for 'fiftieth day'). Luke includes this date from the Jewish festival calendar in the salvation history of (Old Testament) promise and (New Testament) fulfilment. For him,

Pentecost is evidently the day on which the promised Spirit of God descends on humankind. So Pentecost can become the hour of the birth of the Jerusalem community which now overcomes all anxiety, begins with the public testimony to Jesus as Messiah/Son of Man, and has its first missionary success. But in this way Pentecost can also be understood as an event of the constitution of the world-wide church which is potentially present there in its different nations and languages.

Did such a Pentecostal assembly take place historically? Given our sources, that can no longer be decided, but it is quite possible. The first 'assembly' of the followers of Jesus, who (above all) came from Galilee, could well have taken place on the first Pentecost afer Jesus' death, on which no doubt many pilgrims came to Jerusalem. Now according to the Acts of the Apostles even Jesus' mother and brothers were also there. And the constitution of a 'community' of the end-time could have taken place under the influence of the Spirit – in circumstances of charismatic enthusiasm. Possibly Luke took over an already-existing tradition, a tradition of the occurrence of spirit-led mass ecstasy in Jerusalem on the first Pentecost after the crucifixion and resurrection of Jesus.

At all events, that Lukan story of Pentecost impressed itself so strongly on the consciousness of the church that from the fifth century, alongside Easter, people began to celebrate first of all a separate feast of Pentecost fifty days after Easter and then a separate feast of the Ascension forty days after Easter. In contrast to that earlier fifty-day period of joy in which resurrection, ascension and the sending of the Spirit were celebrated simultaneously, now a new historicizing understanding of successive feasts increasingly took root. Indeed, with a reference back to chronological pointers in the Bible the celebration of Easter was finally extended over the whole year to form the 'church's year' (a term from the sixteenth century): an annual liturgical cycle composed of feasts first of Christ and then of the saints. Different beginnings to this cycle of the church's year were still known in the Middle Ages: Easter, or the Annunciation, or particularly Christmas, which was similarly celebrated from the fourth century on. Only in recent times did the beginning on the first Sunday in Advent become established.

'But it's not the church's year that is the decisive question,' I can hear someone object. 'Rather, the decisive question for many contemporaries is: what should the church be now? Should we still remain in the church?'

4. Should we remain in the church?

It's a commonplace that the church today is in a dramatic and deep-seated crisis of credibility, indeed legitimacy. Of course this doesn't just affect the Catholic Church: the Protestant churches are suffering in many ways from a loss of substance and profile, and thus from a still greater loss of members and church attenders. But because of its renewed rigidity, the hierarchical desire to rule, a 'teaching authority' which is incapable of learning and its suppression of the freedom of Christians, the Catholic Church is even more under fire from public criticism. A look at books currently on sale indicates this as a glance. Best-sellers in Germany describe the *Criminal History of Christianity* (K.Deschner) or have as their theme the fatal relationship between church and sexuality (U.Ranke-Heinemann, G.Denzler). One book which has been an international best-seller for a long time culminates in the theory that Pope John Paul I was murdered, and has the provocative title *In God's Name?* (David A.Yallop). This particular book isn't striking because of the murder hypothesis that it puts forward. It is striking because there are evidently millions of people all over the world who believe that certain circles of the Catholic Church are in God's name engaged in shady financial manipulations and have links with criminal organizations (which is unfortunately the case), and will also, if necessary, resort to violence and murder (which cannot be proved and in my view is also improbable).

However, statistics give a more precise answer. World-wide the pastoral work of the Catholic Church is in decline because of the devastating lack of priests. In 1990 one could read even in the Vatican organ, the *Osservatore Romano*, that the process of superannuation in the priesthood in the last ten years has accelerated by almost 360%, and that of 212,500 pastorates world-wide, 53,100 are unoccupied.[46] Moreover since the middle of the 1960s, i.e. since the end of the Second Vatican Council, the number of priests has declined dramatically. It has been estimated that more than 100,000 have married in the meantime.

This situation is reflected specifically in the super-rich and over-organized German church. Of the at present 27.1 million Catholics in the Federal Republic in 1990, a whole 6.5 million, i.e. 24.4%, still go to church regularly. Even the officious Catholic church press now publishes articles about the church in the year 2000 with headlines like 'Community without Priests'.[47] Here is a key sentence: 'The lack of priests in the Catholic church has increased dramatically. For a long time now it has been impossible to fill all the vacant positions.' But instead of finally abolishing the unbiblical and inhuman mediaeval law of celibacy and allowing married and indeed women priests, there is now a desperate appeal to the laity, and illusory pastoral plans are being produced under which pastors are collapsing, while not even lay theologians are being given the necessary authority. All in all, this is a policy of pastoral catastrophe for which the episcopal authorities must answer to God and history, like their blind predecessors at the time of the Reformation.

Let's have no illusions: many people see the church, at least in Germany, as a machine which so far has been well oiled by church taxes and functions smoothly like a great bureaucracy, but which largely lacks a soul because the Spirit has gone out of it. Today this Spirit often seems to have settled outside (or below) the institutional church – in a whole network of groups of every possible kind: Bible groups, youth groups and meditation circles, or peace groups and eco-groups, extending as far as communities inspired by India or the Far East. And even many who remain loyal to their church have long opposed the official course of the hierarchy on decisive questions. According to the survey 'Crisis of Confidence in the Church?', commissioned by the German Conference of Bishops in 1989, only 16% of German Catholics unconditionally accept the unfallibility of the pope, 23% are still against any form of termination of pregnancy, and only 8% still against artificial birth control; 70% would set themselves above papal decisions.[48]

And the more people have to look on while the present Catholic hierarchy, blind to reality, rules over their heads, and forces bishops on them who are not pastors but governors obedient to

Rome, find that their consciences are to be gagged in questions of sexual morality and women are still to be discriminated against, the more Catholic Christian men and women will face the question which many Protestants have long since answered in the negative: 'Why remain in the church? Why not leave, like so many people before us? Can't one follow Jesus without being bound to an institution the support of which involves complicity in the distress which is at present so dominant at present? Can't leaving it be an act of honesty, of courage, of protest or simply even of necessity and disgust?'

Here I shall simply repeat the answer I have given countless times to this question. Much as I personally understand the reasons of any individual for leaving the church and indeed the ministry of the church to devote themselves to other tasks, this is something that I could never do for myself. I have constantly attempted to affirm the community of believers, for all its weaknesses and all its failures. I have always had the feeling that to get out of the church boat – which for many people is an act of honesty and protest – would for me personally be an act of failure and capitulation. Having been in it in better hours, am I to abandon the boat in the storm and leave steering against the wind, bailing it out and possibly the struggle for spiritual survival to others with whom I have previously kept company? No – despite everything, I have received too much in the community of faith in which I grew up to be able to get out of it so simply. I have committed myself too much to change and renewal now to disappoint those who have committed themselves with me. I wouldn't want to give this pleasure to the opponents of renewal or this grief to my friends. I have no time for an élitist Christianity which wants to be better than the many who are there, and no time for church utopias aimed at an ideal community of pure, like-minded people. Despite all my sorry experiences with my church, I believe that critical loyalty is worthwhile, that resistance is meaningful and renewal possible, and that another positive turn in church history cannot be ruled out. But that presupposes that we know what the church is. Hence the question:

5. What is the church?

We can talk meaningfully about 'the church' today only if right from the beginning we are clear that the church is in no way to be identified with 'the hierarchy'. For hierarchy means 'holy rule'! And that is precisely what there is not to be in the church, which is why this word doesn't occur in the New Testament at all. A fundamentally different word appears in the New Testament: *diakonia*. And *diakonia* means 'service'. In other words, power is exercised everywhere, in the church as well, and there is no objection to that in principle. However, in the spirit of Jesus power is never to become rule, but is in principle to be exercised for service. People today have become very sensitive to this and immediately feel whether their pastor, bishop or pope wants to serve or to rule (even 'in God's name') and dominate – so as in fact to retain power and even extend it. Happily, there are not a few pastors at all levels who are credible as servants of their faithful.

A second point: according to the Apostles' Creed Christians do not need to believe 'in' the church. Really? No, they do not, since in that case they would be attaching too much importance to the church; at most one could say that only in a very vague sense. It is striking that already in the Apostles' Creed we find 'I believe *in* God, *in* Jesus Christ, *in* the Holy Spirit', but then 'I believe the church'. This distinction should be noticed: it is more than a linguistic nuance. It gives theological expression to the fundamental difference between God – Father, Son and Spirit – on the one hand and the church on the other, a difference which must not be blurred. The church is almost always named in the third article of the Creed in connection with belief in the Holy Spirit. The original third baptismal question in the earliest church order that we have (the *Apostolic Tradition* of Hippolytus of Rome, from around 215, significantly earlier than the Apostles' Creed) is particularly illuminating. It is very precise: 'Do you also believe *in* the Holy Spirit *within* the holy church for the resurrection of the flesh?' That is in fact decisive: a Christian believes *in* God and *in* the Holy Spirit; by contrast, the church as a human community is only the place where the Spirit of God works, or should work, through human beings.

So what does 'church' mean? Church, briefly and quite traditionally defined in terms of its literal Hebrew-Greek meaning, is 'assembly', 'community', i.e. the fellowship, communion, of those who believe in Jesus as the Christ. It can also be described in a different way: the church is the fellowship of those who have committed themselves to the cause of Jesus Christ and attest it as a hope for all people. Before Easter, as we heard, there was only an eschatological collective inspired by Jesus himself. Only since Easter has there been a commmunity in the name of Jesus Christ, though equally orientated on the end-time. Its foundation is not primarily its own cult, its own constitution, its own organization with specific offices, but solely the confession in faith of this Jesus as the Messiah (Greek *Christos*).

But what should the basic functions be in this church? They are indicated from the beginning: its prime function is the proclamation of the Christian message – the gospel and not some kind of 'world-view' (usually conservative). And for incorporation into the community of those who believe in Christ there is baptism – since Jesus had himself baptized by John the Baptist – but now administered in the name of Jesus, and also of the Father and the Spirit. Furthermore, in memory of him, his last supper and his death, there is the constantly renewed meal of thanksgiving, the eucharist. And in connection both with baptism and the eucharist there is also the constantly renewed promise of the forgiveness of sins and finally the daily service of fellow men and women and of society. From of old all this has had only one aim: to serve the cause of Jesus Christ, at least not to obstruct it, but to advocate it in his Spirit in present-day society, to actualize it, to realize it above all in one's own sphere. Does the church, do the churches, do this today? Churches which often do not have intercommunion with one another?

When they hear the word church, Protestant, Evangelical Christians think first of the local church, and Catholics of the whole church. But both today know that the word church ('*ekklesia*') means both the local church and the whole church at the same time. Here in the biblical understanding the local church is not just, as people would have it in Rome, a 'section' or a subordinate 'province' of the whole church which can be dominated from a centre: the whole church isn't the Roman empire.

133

Conversely, however, the whole church isn't just an accumulation or 'association' of local churches, as it is understood to be in some Protestant communities. No, every local community in Europe, America, Asia or Africa, however small, insignificant, mediocre, indeed pitiful, fully makes present, manifests and represents the whole church of Jesus Christ; all the essential basic functions which I have just mentioned are to be found in it. So the biblical images of the church hold for both the whole church and the local church. In the biblical understanding the local church is already the people of God, the body of Christ, the temple of the Holy Spirit.

'But,' contemporaries ask in an age of democracy, 'isn't the church from the beginning an utterly undemocratic structure, which for that very reason no longer fits in our time?'

6. The church – apostolic but undemocratic?

It is too evident to need proof here that the churches – often persisting spiritually, theologically and organizationally in former paradigms – are all too often authoritarian and sometimes even totalitarian institutions. But according to the New Testament, the church is to be a community in freedom and equality, a community of brothers and sisters: that means, in things great and small, a community of people who are free and in principle equal. Indeed, according to Paul, in Christ there are to be 'neither slave nor free, neither man nor woman' (Gal.3.28). And if the sisters today had a position and significance even remotely resembling their position and significance in the community of Jesus' disciples or in the Pauline communities, then the status and equal rights of women in the church and its offices – especially in the Catholic and Orthodox churches – would be very different. But the sensation caused by the election of the first Lutheran woman bishop in history, in Hamburg in March 1992 (before that there had already been the consecration of an Anglican woman bishop in the USA), shows how slowly completely equal rights for women are being established even in Protestantism.

Certainly there are also countless differences in the church – and should be: not only of persons but also of functions; many kinds of superordination and subordination determined by functions. The church too cannot do without human authority, ministries ('offices') at local, regional, national or universal level. But this authority – of whatever kind – is exercised legitimately only where it is grounded in service and not on force, manifest or hidden, or on ancient, mediaeval or modern privileges. So rather than speaking of church 'office' we would do better to use precise biblical terminology and speak of church 'ministry': of many and very varied 'ministries' or 'charisms', which especially means callings. However, the main thing is not the terminology, but what happens in practice.

The church may not be an aristocracy or even a monarchy, although some people act as if it was. A church which goes by the original church of the apostles would be a democratic community in the best sense of the word. Here the democratic element in the church does not of course relate to the question of truth, as is suspected particularly by Catholic traditionalists, who vehemently combat and reject the concept of a church as a democratic community. As if there could ever be a church as a democratic community which would decide by majority vote on what was to be regarded as truth or untruth, as revelation or human work, the Word of God or the voice of the people. Of course all members and groups in the church stand under the Word of God. Strictly speaking, it is not the people but the Word of God, Christ, the Lord himself, who should rule in the church. And the people cannot be a substitute for revelation any more than the hierarchy can. No, for the church to be 'a democratic community' is simply and solely a matter of how it organizes and structures its service under God's Word, in the Spirit of Jesus. So 'democracy' doesn't mean surrendering the church to the spirit of the age and putting truth to the vote, but corresponds to the New Testament constitution of the church, according to which all in the church are called equally to service, though in different functions.

'But what then becomes of the apostolic foundation of the church?', some people may ask here. 'Didn't the appeal to the apostles lead to a division in the church between clergy and laity, between those who are followers of the apostles and the mass of those who are to follow the followers?' The answer is that apostolic succession in the church is not a special privilege of a few who are called, but the task of the whole church. A church may be regarded as apostolic only if it lives quite generally in the apostolic succession, i.e. in accord with the apostolic testimony as it has come down in the New Testament. And this testimony becomes concrete in the constant exercising of apostolic ministry. This apostolic ministry is no introverted navel-gazing by the communities, but proclamation and presence of Christians in the world. And only to the degree that the services of leadership, not just those of bishops but also those of priests and pastors generally, in accord with the apostolic testimony, continue the task of founding and leading the church, is it possible to speak of a special 'apostolic succession' of these particular services of leadership, understood functionally. People normally enter them by vocation and the laying on of hands by the church leaders (with the participation of the community), but this isn't the only way. According to agreed ecumenical documents, a mutual recognition of church ministries in the divided churches is not only theologically justifiable but even pastorally desirable.

So 'apostolic succession' is not a special privilege which may be the basis for hierarchical arrogance and division in the church: it is the invitation to all Christians in the church to become 'more apostolic', i.e to strive to be loyal to the origin of the church. That applies especially to those entrusted with special services of leadership.

'But the Apostles' Creed doesn't just speak of the apostolic church but also of the "catholic church". Does that then mean that only the Catholic Church is the true church in the sense of the Creed?' The answer is that this is the one and only point at which the Protestant, Evangelical Confession differs from the Catholic in the new German version: I believe 'the Christian' or the 'universal Christian' church. But:

7. What does catholic mean today? What does evangelical mean?

For the majority of Catholics and Protestants, the traditional doctrinal differences from the sixteenth century – scripture and tradition, sin and grace, faith and works, eucharist and priesthood, church and papacy – are no longer reasons for splitting the church.

In fact these differences have long been worked through by an ecumenical theology of Catholic or Evangelical, Protestant origin. People aren't theologically conformist in all matters, but they do agree that the abiding differences no longer justify a split in the church. So many Catholics and Protestants are waiting for the church leaders in Rome and elsewhere finally, at long last, to follow the insights of so many offical ecumenical commissions which have long since achieved theological agreement on these points and to put them into practice. In the epoch-making shift from modernity to post-modernity, it just will not do for the Catholic Church still to be stuck in problems of the Middle Ages (the autocracy of the pope, Marian dogmas, the veneration of the saints), or the Evangelical, Protestant church still to be stuck in problems from the time of the Reformation (resentment of authority, tradition and sacraments – especially the eucharist). The decisive difference between 'Catholic' and 'Protestant' lies in different basic attitudes which have developed since the Reformation, but today the one-sidedness of these attitudes has been overcome, and they can be integrated into a true ecumenicity. What does that mean? What do 'Catholic' and 'Evangelical' church (i.e. the church of Protestants) originally mean?

In origin, 'catholic church' means quite unpolemically the whole, universal church as distinct from the local church. Even today, the *Ecclesia catholica* of the Creed does not denote any confessional church, and despite its size even the Roman Catholic Church becomes a particular confessional church by the addition 'Roman', which has become customary only in recent times. 'Catholic church' really means the whole, universal, comprehensive church. Like 'Anglo Catholic', 'Roman Catholic' is strictly speaking a contradiction in terms: particular-universal = wooden iron.

So who can call themselves catholics? Only those are basically catholic in attitude, those who are particularly concerned with the catholic = whole, universal, world-wide church. To be specific, catholics are those who are concerned with the continuity of faith and the community of faith in time (the two-thousand-year-old tradition), which has been maintained through all the breaks, and secondly with the universality of faith and the community of faith in space, which embraces all groups, nations, races and classes.

The opposite of such Catholicity would be 'Protestant' particularism and radicalism, from which authentic evangelical radicalism and relatedness to the community are clearly distinct.

So what does 'evangelical church' mean? It means the church which is primarily orientated on the *evangelium Christi*, the gospel of Jesus Christ himself. That does not exclude tradition, but quite decisively subordinates it to the gospel, which remains the normative authority (*norma normans*) for all authorities in the church.

So who may call themselves evangelical? Only those have a fundamentally evangelical attitude, who think it important constantly to submit all church traditions, doctrines and practices especially to criticism in the light of the gospel (originally laid down in Holy Scripture) and, secondly, are concerned with constant practical reform in accordance with the norms of this gospel (*ecclesia semper reformanda*). Such an evangelical attitude contrasts with 'Roman Catholic' traditionalism and syncretism, which has nothing to do with authentically catholic tradition and breadth.

– Now if the two basic attitudes – the truly catholic and the truly evangelical – are brought together, it follows from what I have said so far that, rightly understood, the basic catholic and evangelical attitudes are in no way exclusive. Specifically:

– Today the baptized Catholic can also have a truly evangelical disposition.

– Conversely, the baptized Evangelical (i.e. Protestant) can show a truly catholic breadth.

– Today countless Christian men and women, male and female pastors, and often communities throughout the world (despite the resistance in church apparatus and the power-thinking of church functionaries) in fact live by an 'evangelical catholicity' or – the other way round, but it is the same thing – 'catholic evangelicity', a constant concern for catholic breadth, centred on the gospel and always in need of further correction. And what a historical opportunity has been missed by Rome now that, after the great ecumenical breakthrough of the Second Vatican Council in the 1960s and the working out of countless consensus documents in the 1970s, in the 1980s and 1990s it has come to a complete ecumenical standstill under the pope from Poland – one which is merely concealed by ecumenical speeches and gestures. That is a consequence not only of the person but above all of the institution – just one sign of how the mediaeval absolutist papacy needs radical reform in the evangeical spirit.

Nevertheless, today already countless Catholics, Protestants, Anglicans and Orthodox, and also some Catholic, Protestant, Anglican and probably also Orthodox communities are practising real ecumenicity. In this way Christians today can be Christians in the full sense without denying their own confessional past, but also without getting in the way of a better ecumenical future. There is no overlooking the fact that for a growing number of our contemporaries, being a true Christian means being an ecumenical Christian.

'I could certainly agree with that,' someone will say, 'but the least credible attribute of the church is probably holiness. *Credo sanctam ecclesiam* – the holy church? Surely that's more illusion than reality?' Hence the question:

8. A 'holy' church?

If we consider the real church realistically, first of all, without any ifs and buts, we have to say that it is a sinful church, because it consists of fallible, sinful people. This statement is so much a matter of course today that it is quite superfluous to remind contemporaries of all the wrong historical decisions and developments; all the personal failure and personal guilt, particularly of those in office; all the imperfections, deficiencies and disfigurements. Indeed, whether it is a matter of discrimination against women and the burning of witches; of the persecution of theologians and heretics; of anti-Judaism and pogroms of the Jews; of Renaissance popes; or the cases of Hus, Luther, Descartes, Giordano Bruno, Galileo, Kant, Loisy, Teilhard de Chardin and so many others, no Christians should be shy about speaking of often incredible blindness, terrifying sin and many-sided blasphemy even in the church – in their church.

What is involved here is not just the failure of the human individual as such but also the inhumanity of many church structures, and indeed also that evil which transcends the failure of the individual in a power which must be called demonic and which moreover inevitably leads to a perversion of what is Christian. For that we do not need the 'criminal history of Christianity' which is constantly rewritten. Who has not experienced enough in his or her own biography to be able to say that all in all, church history is not only a very human history but also a deeply sinful history? And it was so from the beginning. One has only to read the New Testament letters to be faced with the sorry reality of guilt and sin. So:

– No more of the evasions in which theologians constantly take refuge when confronted with this alienating, painful, shaming evidence of a sinful church;

– No pseudo-holy segregation of the 'holy' members, as has been attempted by some sectarian groups of the early, mediaeval and modern church and recently by Opus Dei, with its clerical-Fascist origin. They all want to exclude the 'sinful' members from the church so that only the spiritual elite, the sinless, the pure, the holy are left. But who will then really be left, if we are honest?

– No threadbare distinction between the 'holy' church and sinful believers, where in order not to compromise the holiness of 'the church', a completely abstract distinction is made between the members and the church itself, which allegedly remains sinless. But there is no such thing as an abstract church – it is only there in concrete!

No, none of these expedients helps. Reality has to be taken into account. The church is a church of sinners and therefore a sinful church. But conversely, it follows from this insight that the holiness of the church is manifestly not grounded in its members and their moral and religious actions and attitudes.

But what does 'holy' in fact mean? In both the Old and New Testaments, 'holy' means being set apart by God and for God, in contrast to the 'pro-fane' ('lying before the *fanum*, the holy place'). Strikingly, there is never any talk in the New Testament of a 'holy' church. But all through it there is mention of communities which as such are called 'the saints' ('the holy ones'), described as a 'holy people' or a 'holy temple' of which believers are the living stones. In contrast to Old Testament Israel, it is striking that here material holiness fades into the background. In the New Testament there are no separate holy spheres and objects. Even baptism and the eucharist are not called 'holy'; they do not themselves create holiness in some magical automatic way: they are utterly dependent on the holy God on the one side and the response of believers on the other. There is no mention in the New Testament of an institutional holiness, of a church which gives as many as possible of its institutions and persons, its places, times and vessels the attribute 'holy'. If the New Testament is concerned with holiness at all, it is concerned with an utterly personal holiness, a basic attitude of 'holiness' for each individual, which means a total orientation on the will of the 'holy God' himself.

The conclusion to be drawn is that the specific community of faith which calls itself the church is thus holy and sinful at the same time. It is the battlefield between God's Spirit and the demon of evil in the world, and the front does not run simply between the holy church and the unholy world, but right through the middle of the human heart.

'But if that is so,' a contemporary will ask here, 'how can we still speak of a *communio sanctorum*, as happens in the Creed? In these circumstances, hasn't the term "communion of saints" become meaningless?'

9. What does 'communion of saints' mean?

It has already become clear that from the New Testament perspective the 'communion of saints' (*communio sanctorum*) is simply to be understood as the community of believers (*communio fidelium*). This is just another way of describing the church. These 'saints' are anything but exalted ideal figures. What is meant are saints without haloes: believers who still have their failings and sins yet who through God's call in Christ have forsworn the sinful world and are attempting in everyday life, for better or worse, to follow the way of Christ's disciples. These, then, are no self-made saints, but are only 'called to be saints' (I Cor.1.2), 'saints in Christ Jesus' (Phil.1.1), 'holy and beloved elect' (Col.3.12). So the church may be called 'holy' only to the degree that it is called by God himself through Christ in the Spirit as the community of believers and has placed itself at his service, raised above the banality of the world's course by God's liberating concern. God himself, in so far as he gains power over human hearts and establishes his rule as the Holy Spirit, is the foundation of the community of saints.

Now the fact cannot be overlooked that in the Apostles' Creed the 'communion of saints' is not just an apposition, an addition to the 'holy catholic church'. Strikingly, this formula appears as an addition to the Creed only around 400 (with Nicetas of Remesiana). In the course of the fifth century it also found its way into the Roman Creed, the Apostles' Creed, by way of Gallican-Spanish creeds. But that leads quite clearly to two possible interpretations which go beyond the 'communion of saints' as the 'community of believers'.

– Because the second word of the Latin phrase *communio sanctorum* can also be understood as neuter, the phrase can mean participation in the holy things (*sancta*) in the earthly church, i.e. in the sacraments, then with a particular reference to the eucharist as the centre of liturgical life.

– But 'communion of saints' can also mean communion with the saints (*sancti*) in heaven, i.e. with the martyrs and other righteous of all times, whom we may believe to be in God's consummation. So they are as it were guarantors of the future consummation of all Christians. The regular translation 'communion of saints' clearly opts for this second meaning.

But I can hear an interruption: 'Surely you don't want us contemporaries of the twentieth century, including Protestants, to endorse a mediaeval veneration of the saints and Mary in the spirit of conservative Roman Catholicism? Does one have to venerate the saints, and especially Mary, to be a Christian?'

The answer to this can be relatively brief. Even according to sixteenth-century Council of Trent the veneration of the saints is not a 'must' for the traditional Catholic of the Counter-Reformation. The claim is only that such veneration of the saints is good and useful.[49] Nowhere is it said that to venerate the saints is a duty or even necessary for salvation. And it was already established by the Second Council of Nicaea in 787, against the 'iconoclasts', those in the Eastern Church who destroyed idols, that there is an essential difference between the veneration of the saints and the worship which is due to God alone. Moreover, the distinction between *veneratio*, veneration (in respect of saints), and *adoratio*, worship (due only to God in his Christ), was then also constantly maintained in the Western Catholic Church.

Now the veneration of particular martyrs (from as early as the second century) and then also of prominent non-martyrs, 'confessors' (from the end of the fourth century), originally came from the grass roots of the church below, being spontaneously initiated by believers themselves. Only over a period of time did bishops and finally – in connection with Roman centralization after the tenth/eleventh centuries – Rome adopt beatification ('canonization'), which ultimately, in good Roman fashion, led to a precisely regulated legal procedure, to processes of canonization in which 'miracles' (recently also 'moral' ones) still play a special and not unproblematical role. Only one who is given the 'honour of altars', i.e. the nomination to veneration and intercession within the framework of the official liturgy, may legitimately be called 'holy' or a 'saint'. It is well known how the veneration of the saints in the late Middle Ages led to tremendous abuses (the cult of relics, indulgences, curial financing). It is therefore more than understandable that the Reformers should have subjected the veneration of the saints to sharp criticism, and indeed that Calvin and the Reformed radicals rejected them.

We cannot simply blame the Holy Spirit for the fact that in the past ten centuries twice as many men as women have been canonized, only 76 laity as opposed to 303 clergy and nuns, and that hardly any happily married figures appear but at best widows. The present pope, too, has rediscovered beatification and canonization as an instrument of his restorative church policy orientated on the Middle Ages. Here the self-righteousness of the hierarchy became particularly blatant in the beatification of Edith Stein. This Jewish woman was used for a triumphal self-promotion of the Catholic hierarchy, without a word of self-criticism about the complete failure of this hierachy at a time when Edith Stein, too, was carried off to be gassed in a Nazi concentration camp, not because she was a Catholic nun but because she was Jewish.

Nevertheless, even today the notion of 'saints' isn't completely meaningless. Individual Protestants, too, argue for an 'evangelical veneration of the saints', though in the moderate line from Martin Luther on, conditions are attached to this. These conditions are also important for Catholics. If there is veneration of the saints, this must not be at the expense of God or Christ. A decentralization of faith is unacceptable. The veneration of particular saints can strengthen faith. Concrete examples of discipleship of Christ can provide guidelines for living. The inclusion of the great history of discipleship of Christ can create solidarity over the ages.

That indulgences have now largely disappeared from the Catholic church and that the cult of relics has been pushed firmly into the background helps not only ecumenical understanding but also Catholic spirituality. Conversely, there is no mistaking the fact that figures like Francis of Assisi and Thomas More, Hildegard of Bingen or Teresa of Avila, have also stimulated some Protestant Christians in their practice of the Christian life. And why shouldn't some living figures from the two-thousand-year history of the church – of course this also goes for authentically evangelical figures like Dietrich Bonhoeffer or Martin Luther King – say just as much to us as figures of the Bible who are at best known in sketchy outline?

But one thing is clear today: it is no longer the intercession and imitation of canonized saints that now stands at the centre of theological and church interest in reflections on the *communio sanctorum*, but again that 'community of saints' as understood in the New Testament, in which believers share on the basis of baptism. But the theme of the 'communion of saints', the 'holiness' of the church, cannot be discussed without asking about the relationship in each individual between 'holiness' and 'sin'.

Many contemporaries tend to react particularly allergically to talk of guilt and sin in particular: 'Hasn't the church done infinite damage by its fixation on sin, particularly in the sexual sphere, which has thoroughly obscured the whole "good news"?' But at least the Creed doesn't focus on the production and perpetuation of guilt feelings and guilt complexes, but quite the opposite, on the forgiveness of guilt.

10. What does 'forgiveness of sins' mean?

There is no doubt that in our contemporary society there is a tendency to deny, to repress, to fob off guilt, to reduce it to what can be proved legally. Here not only political and financial scandals of an almost unprecedented extent in civilized states, but above all the tragedies of our century, have made all too clear the many dimensions of guilt – Urs Baumann and Karl-Josef Kuschel have reflected on this in the light of both literature and theology.[50] Here there are not only the individual and psychological dimensions of guilt but also its social, historical, structural and ecological dimensions. Modern literature in particular (from Kafka and Camus to Frisch) makes it clear that no one (whether or not he or she believes in God) is spared experiences of helplessness, failure and guilt. Everyone – whether religious or not – is entangled in complex histories of guilt which they would like to repress or deny. Conversely, however, representatives of the church have instilled guilt-feelings in people in a very narrow field, that of sexuality, while being very generous in other spheres (allowing wars, sanctioning colonialism and economic exploitation). So a self-critical Christian theology will attack both the repression of guilt in society and the church's production of guilt feelings in the wrong place or with a one-sided fixation. The goal here is not the perpetuation of guilt, but liberation from it: 'The goal of the Christian overcoming of guilt is not condemnation but the acquittal of the sinner, the "therapy" of guilt.'[51]

The Creed doesn't spend a long time on a general theory of evil, the origin of which has never been explained satisfactorily, nor on an anthropology or sociology of sin, which clearly shouldn't be a central issue for faith. The Creed immediately places a positive emphasis: it presupposes the sinfulness of human beings, but at the same time speaks of the possibility of forgiving sins. But how is this to be understood in the light of the New Testament and in connection with present-day problems?

This theological accent points back to the proclamation and conduct of Jesus himself. For in the case of Jesus it is already striking that his proclamation of the kingdom of God resolutely calls for *metanoia*, turning back from a false, sinful way. But here Jesus never meant to produce guilt feelings and leave people alone with them, or to oppress them, to make them do penance in sackcloth and ashes. What he meant, rather, was to invite them to an inner, radical and total conversion and homecoming of the whole person to God and to a life lived for fellow human beings. And this invitation also goes out to the pious and righteous who do not think that they need repentance, and still more to those who are criticized, rejected and repudiated by the pious: the lost sons and daughters. Jesus isn't concerned with supposed insults to God and his law but with people who have become guilty and unhappy; he doesn't want to condemn and punish them but to liberate them and integrate them afresh into the community.

In the case of Jesus it is also striking that to the scandal of the pious he offers fellowship to all 'sinners' and quite specifically eats and drinks with them. Indeed, according to the testimony of the Gospels, though this can hardly be verified historically, he even dares explicitly to promise human beings the forgivess of their sins. In so doing, however, he put himself outside the law as it stood, which calls for the punishment of the sinner. Indeed, in so doing he claims what according to Jewish faith is due to God alone: 'Who can forgive sins but God alone?' (Mark 2.7). However, it is said there that the people 'praised God who had given such authority to men' (Matt.9.8).

Here already it becomes clear that when Jesus talks about the forgiveness of sins he is concerned to make his joyful, liberating message concrete. Jesus was no gloomy preacher of punishment who enjoyed pointing out people's sins to them. All *metanoia*, all repentance, all 'penance' is offered people as a new, positive possibility. According to the whole of the New Testament it has nothing gloomy and negative about it, as later church penitential practice often suggested when it was thought that the grace of God had to be earned by works of penance. No, the decisive thing about the New Testament is that conversion already comes through God's grace and presupposes God's forgiveness. It is not the consequence of an oppressive law, which only demands and cannot provide fulfilment: 'You must!' It is a consequence of the gospel, the good, joyful message of the offer of God's grace which offers people forgiveness without conditions and makes conversion possible: 'You may!' And we all know what a liberating, indeed cheering, experience it can be if after an action which was clearly wrong, perhaps wicked (after a lie, a breach of trust, of loyalty), we hear from the person involved, by a word or a gesture: 'Whatever has happened has happened and cannot be undone; put a line under it; you are forgiven, everything's all right!'

In the light of the New Testament, penance must not be limited to the performance of particular penitential acts. Baptism, which was originally adult baptism, is fundamental. It happens 'for the forgiveness of sins' and is meant to make possible a real new beginning. But it is also clear that the act of baptism doesn't produce any magic sinlessness. Temptation and tribulation remain. We shall always ask to be delivered from evil; we shall always ask for forgiveness.

Forgiveness can come about in many ways. So in the light of the gospel the various historical forms of forgiveness of sins are to be relativized, and none of the forms which have grown up in history is to be canonized once and for all. Forgiveness of sins is possible:

– through baptism, as we heard, which is performed 'for the forgiveness of sins';
– also through the preaching of the gospel itself;
– also through the general absolution in the liturgy, but also by possible absolution from any believer;
– finally, by the special absolution of ministers, which has become the norm above all in the Catholic Church.

It was only with time that the forgiveness of sins became the privilege of bishops. A public 'second penance' after baptism was necessary for sins which cut a person off from the church (apostasy, murder, public adultery) until being received back by the bishop after the time of penance. It was only after the sixth/seventh centuries that the possibility of repeating penance for lesser sins as well, and thus private penance with absolution through the priest, was introduced from Ireland and Scotland; this was so-called auricular penance, which was prescribed in the high Middle Ages for 'serious' sins and for many reasons has drastically declined in most recent times.

However, in the perspective of Jesus something else is more important than the forms of 'sacramental' penance which developed only over time: the forgiveness received by God is to be passed on to others. I have to acknowledge that it was only in the course of Christian-Jewish dialogue that the meaning of Jesus' parable of the generous king who forgives his minister a giant debt, without this minister feeling prompted to forgive his debtors their debts, first dawned on me. According to this parable, Jesus condemns the action of the minister with unusual sharpness, because he threw his own debtors into prison.

Let's not delude ourselves: the forgiveness of guilt between people is by no means 'natural'; it isn't at all something to be taken for granted. How could it be, say in the face of a public slander, a tremendous injury, the murder of an individual or even a horrific genocide like the Holocaust? And there can be no question but that as Christians we have to do everything possible to see that such a cruel event is never forgotten. Moreover, talk of the forgiveness of sins itself must be protected against encouraging forgetfulness (or even repression). But for that very reason, may not the Holocaust also be forgiven? Quite often one hears in dialogue with Jews that forgiving is not for human beings, but is solely God's affair! Only God can forgive guilt – and this particular guilt.

But what would that mean? I ask that out of a concern for understanding between Jews and Christians, out of a concern for the relationship betwen Germans and Jews, Jews and Palestinians. It would mean that there can be no reconciliation between individuals and peoples, that they must endure an eternal guilt – until the end of the world. In this way, for example, the German guilt towards the Jews could never end – either in this generation or in the next. That cannot be the solution! And precisely in the light of the message of the 'forgiveness of sins' this need not be the solution.

Now certainly the Hebrew Bible does not call for forgiveness of one person by another. But there are at least isolated instances of it in the Talmud. Indeed, in the book of Jesus Ben Sira from the second century BCE (though this has only been handed down in a Greek translation and is therefore non-canonical) we read: 'Remember the end of your life, and cease from enmity . . . remember the covenant of the Most High, and forgive guilt' (Sir.28.6f.).

But how often have even Christians failed to forgive one another's guilt and that of yet others? And how often in the course of the centuries have there been calls for vengeance between 'Christian nations' instead of forgiveness, which inevitably led to a hardening of peoples' hearts, to constantly new hatred, and ultimately to new bloodshed and wars! That is evident from that irreconcilable 'ancestral enmity' between France and Germany which was dominated by ideas of mutual revenge – resulting in three major wars and many times the six million Jewish victims of the Holocaust!

My question is whether in this situation the message of Jesus in particular about the forgiveness of sins could not be a challenge to Jews and above all to Christians, a challenge to a spiritual renewal and change of heart, which would also have the greatest political consequences. For Jesus lays down the requirement, not just somewhere, incidentally, but quite centrally, that there can be no reconciliation with God without reconciliation in the interpersonal sphere. Divine forgiveness is bound up with forgiveness between human beings! So in the Our Father, after the petitions for the coming of the kingdom of God and the doing of God's will we find the petition, 'Forgive us our trespasses as we forgive those who trespass against us' (Matt.6.12). And that is emphasized further: 'For if you forgive men their transgressions, so your heavenly Father will also forgive you. But if you do not forgive men, your Father will not forgive your transgressions either' (Matt.6.14f.). Human beings cannot receive God's great forgiveness and then refuse lesser forgiveness to fellow human beings: they must pass on the forgiveness that they have received. That is the meaning of the parable of the generous king and the meaning of the provocative saying that people are not to forgive seven times but seventy times seven: time and again, endlessly.

Of course this demand for forgiveness is not to be interpreted legalistically. It doesn't institute a new law on the principle that one is to forgive seventy-seven times but not seventy-eight. So Jesus' demand cannot just be turned into a state law: it doesn't put human courts out of business. However, Jesus' demand *is* a moral appeal to human generosity and warm-heartedness, to individual men and women – but in some circumstances also the representatives of states – in a quite specific situation as it were to get round the law: to forgive and to go on forgiving.

This could be of the utmost significance not only among members of a family, partners in marriage and friends, but also in inter-religious dialogue. What a difference it would make if Christians and Jews, Christians and Muslims, indeed (and in the present situation this is especially explosive) Jews and Muslims would also come together in the spirit of the forgiveness of their sins – their hatred, their enmity, their acts of terror, their wars. In the awareness that the God of Abraham, in whom Jews, Christians and Muslims all believe, is one who is all merciful and whose mercy is to be handed on. Tbe world would look different if Christians, Jews and Muslims learned to deal with one another in the spirit of the 'forgiveness of sins'.

But one last question in this chapter on the Holy Spirit, which one or another critical contemporary has probably put already:

11. Why is there no mention of the Trinity in the Apostles' Creed?

'There is mention of belief in God the Father, in the Son and in the Holy Spirit, but why isn't there a word in this Apostles' Creed about the "triune God", the most Holy Trinity, which some people even call the "central mystery" of Christianity?' At the end of this section on the Holy Spirit we must put this question quite frankly.

The historical evidence is in fact remarkable. The Greek word *trias* first appears in the second century (in the apologist Theophilos), and the Latin *trinitas* only in the third century (with the African Tertullian); the classical doctrine of the Trinity, of 'one divine nature in three persons', even appears only at the end of the fourth century (formulated by the three Cappadocians Basil, Gregory of Nazianzus and Gregory of Nyssa). The feast of the Trinity – which came into being in Gaul and was at first rejected by Rome as the 'festival of a dogma' – was only prescribed at the time of the exile in Avignon by the French Pope John XXII in 1334.

Now no one who reads the New Testament will dispute that throughout it we find Father, Son and Spirit, and it is no coincidence that the liturgical baptismal formula in Matthew is to baptize 'in the name of the Father and of the Son and of the Holy Spirit' (Matt.28.19). But the whole question is how Father, Son and Spirit are related to one another. And strikingly, there is not a single passage anywhere in the New Testament in which it is said that Father, Son and Spirit are 'of one substance', i.e. have a single common divine nature (being, physis, substance). So to this degree it is not surprising that there is no such statement in the Apostles' Creed.

If we want to make this relationship between the three 'entities' comprehensible again for contemporaries today we cannot simply go back to dogmatic formulations of councils stamped with the Hellenistic spirit, which presuppose a very time-conditioned conceptual system. So while the formulas of the councils are not to be thrown away unthinkingly, they are not to be repeated thoughtlessly either; rather, they must be interpreted carefully. We must take the trouble to look at the New Testament, which is still stamped by Judaism and is often closer to us. Then it quickly becomes clear that according to the New Testament, Father, Son and Holy Spirit are three very different entities who do not appear there simply identified schematically and ontologically with a divine nature. Moreover, Jesus himself does not say a single word about a 'central mystery' or 'basic dogma' according to which 'three divine persons' (hypostases, relations, modes of being. . .), Father, Son and Spirit, have 'one divine nature' in common.

A look at Christian iconography can also illustrate the problem here. In Western art there were no inhibitions about portraying the Trinity with the help of three persons, three heads or one head with three faces. Western art also knows the so-called 'mercy seat', a portrayal of the Trinity in which God the Father is depicted as an old man with snow-white hair and a grey beard, holding on his lap the cross, on which the Son hangs, while above them or between them the Holy Spirit hovers in the form of a dove. No wonder, though, that such representations of the Trinity encouraged the idea that Christians believed in something like three gods in heaven, and that belief in the Trinity was thus tritheism in disguise, a charge which Jews and Muslims have constantly raised against Christians and still keep raising.

By contrast, the tradition of the Christian East was far more restrained. In his doctrine of icons, John of Damascus (c.670-750), the last great church father, who is the norm for Orthodoxy, firmly maintained that one cannot make an image of the invisible, incorporeal, indescribable and formless God. Only what is visible of God, i.e. his revelation in Jesus Christ, may be depicted in images. This line of the prohibition of images of the Trinity was maintained in the Orthodox church. Moreover, Andrei Rublov's famous icon (painted between 1422 and 1427), probably in reaction to depictions of the mercy-seat influenced by the West, has only a symbolic representation of the Trinity in the form of three angels as they appeared to Abraham (Gen.18).[52]

The inhibitions of the painters should give us food for thought, though we cannot simply take over the trinitarian theology of Eastern Orthodoxy. We must ask ourselves the question how we should we speak today of Father, Son and Spirit.

12. How do we talk of Father, Son and Spirit?

Here too we do best to keep very close to the New Testament. And in the New Testament there is probably no better story to illustrate the relationship of Father, Son and Spirit than that speech made in his own defence by Stephen the Protomartyr, which Luke has handed down to us in his Acts of the Apostles. During this speech Stephen has a vision: 'Filled with the Holy Spirit, he looked up to heaven and saw the glory of God and Jesus standing at the right hand of God, and said, "Behold, I see heaven opened and the Son of Man standing at the right hand of God" ' (Acts 7.55f.). So here we have mention of God, Jesus the Son of Man, and the Holy Spirit. But Stephen does not see, say, a deity with three faces, far less three identical men, nor any triangular symbol of the kind that was similarly used in Western art. Rather:

– The Holy Spirit is at Stephen's side, is in Stephen himself. The Spirit, the invisible power and might which comes from God, fills him completely and thus opens his eyes: 'in the Spirit' he sees heaven.

– God himself (ho theos – the God) remains hidden, does not have human form; only his 'glory' (Hebrew kabod, Greek doxa) is visible: God's splendour and power, the splendour of light, which emanates fully from him.

– Jesus, finally, visible as the Son of man, stands (and we already know the significance of this formula) 'at the right hand of God', i.e. in throne community, with the same power and glory! Exalted as Son of God and taken up into God's eternal life, he is God's representative for us and at the same time as a human being the representative of human beings before God.

So the relation of Father, Son and Spirit could be described like this:
- God, the invisible Father, *above* us,
- Jesus, the Son of Man, with God *for* us,
- Holy Spirit, from God's power and love, *in* us.

The apostle Paul also sees things in very much the same way: God himself creates salvation *through* Jesus Christ *in* the Spirit. Just as we are also to pray *to* God *through* Jesus Christ in the Spirit: the prayers are directed to God, the Father, himself *per dominum nostrum Jesum Christum*. Jesus as the Lord exalted to God has so much become God's might, power, Spirit that he is not only seized by the Spirit and in the power of the spirit but on the basis of the resurretion is even himself in the mode of existence and activity of the Spirit. And in the Spirit he can be present to believers: not physically and materially present, nor in an unreal way either, but as a spiritual reality in the life of individuals and the community of faith, and there above all in worship, in the celebration of the meal with the breaking of the bread and drinking of the cup, in grateful remembrance of him. So the encounter of 'God', 'Lord' and 'Spirit' is, for believers, ultimately one and the same encounter, God's own action, as for example Paul expresses it in the formula of greeting: 'The grace of the Lord Jesus Christ and the love of God and the fellowship of the Holy Spirit be with you all' (II Cor.13.13).

It was also possible to speak of Father, Son and Spirit in the same way in the farewell discourses in John, where the Spirit has the personal features of a 'support' and 'helper' (this is what 'the other Paraclete' in John 14.15 means, and not e.g. 'comforter'). The Spirit is as it were the representative on earth of the exalted Christ. He is sent by the Father in the name of Jesus. So he does not speak of himself, but simply brings to mind what Jesus himself had said.

It may have become clear from all this that according to the New Testament the key question in the doctrine of the Trinity is not the question which has been declared an impenetrable 'mystery' (*mysterium stricte dictum*), how three so different entities can be ontologically one, but the christological question of how according to scripture the relationship of Jesus (and consequently also that of the Spirit) to God himself can be stated.

Here the belief in the one God which Christianity has in common with Judaism and Islam mustn't be jeopardized for a moment. There is no other God than God. But what is decisive, particularly for dialogue with Jews and Muslims, is the insight that according to the New Testament the principle of unity is clearly not the one divine 'nature' (*physis*) common to a number of entities, as has been supposed since the neo-Nicene theology of the fourth century. For the New Testament, as for the Hebrew Bible, the principle of unity is clearly the one God (*ho theos*: the God = the Father), from whom are all things and to whom are all things.

So according to the New Testament, statements about Father, Son and Spirit are not metaphysical-ontological statements about God in himself and his innermost nature: about a static substance of a triune God resting in himself and not at all open to us. Rather, they are soteriologial, christological statements about how God himself reveals himself through Jesus Christ in this world: about God's dynamic and universal activity in history, about his relationship to human beings and their relationship to him. So for all the difference of roles, they are about a unity of Father, Son and Spirit, namely as an event of revelation and a unity of revelation: God himself is made manifest in the Spirit through Jesus Christ.

The contemporary might ask: 'On these presuppositions may perhaps talk of Father, Son and Spirit perhaps also become easier for Jews and Muslims to understand? In particular, dialogue with Judaism and Islam will become an important touchstone of whether Christians take monotheism seriously.'

I shall try to sum up in three sentences what seems to me to be the biblical nucleus of the traditional doctrine of the Trinity, in the light of the New Testament, considered for today:

– To believe in God the Father means to believe in the one God, creator, preserver and perfecter of the world and humankind: Judaism, Christianity and Islam have this belief in the one God in common.

– To believe in the Holy Spirit means to believe in God's effective might and power in human beings and the world: Jews, Christians and Muslims also have this belief in God's Spirit in common.

– To believe in the Son of God means to believe in the revelation of the one God in the man Jesus of Nazareth who is thus God's Word, Image and Son. This decisive difference needs to be discussed further, particularly among the three prophetic religions.

– Perhaps critical contemporaries might be asked a question in return: 'Do these highly theological statements also mean something quite existential for you, or does this remain simply a "truth of faith", a "dogma", and at best "liturgy", "doxology", praise of God's "glory"?'

13. Spirit of freedom

For me, to believe in the Holy Spirit, the Spirit of God, means to accept in trust that God himself can be inwardly present to me, that as gracious might and power he can rule over my ambivalent disposition, my heart which is often so unfathomable. And what is particularly important to me here is that the Spirit of God is not a spirit which brings slavery. The Spirit is the Spirit of Jesus Christ, the Spirit of freedom. This Spirit of freedom already emanated from the words and deeds of Jesus of Nazareth. His Spirit is now definitively God's Spirit, since the crucified Christ was exalted by God and now lives and rules in God's mode of being, in the Spirit of God. Therefore Paul can quite rightly say, 'Where the Spirit of the Lord is, there is freedom' (II Cor.3.17). And this does not just mean freedom from guilt, legalism and death, but also freedom to act, freedom for life in gratitude, hope and joy. That is so despite all the resistance and compulsion in society and church, despite all the deficiencies in structures and failings of individuals. This Spirit of freedom points me forwards as the Spirit of the future: not to consolation in the beyond, but to preservation in the present.

And because I know that the Holy Spirit is the Spirit of Jesus Christ, I also have a firm criterion for testing and discerning the spirits. God's Spirit can no longer be misused here as an obscure, nameless divine power which is easy to misinterpret. No, God's Spirit is quite clearly the Spirit of Jesus Christ. And in quite concrete and practical terms that means that there can be no hierarchy nor any theology nor any enthusiasm which seeks to appeal to the 'Holy Spirit' over Jesus Christ, which can claim the Spirit of Jesus Christ for themselves. That is where any office, obedience, any involvement in theology, church and society finds its limits.

For me, to believe in the Holy Spirit, the Spirit of Jesus Christ, especially in the face of many charismatic and pneumatic movements, means that the Spirit is never my own possibility but always power, might, gift of God, to be received in believing trust. So the Spirit is no unholy spirit of the time, of the church, of offices or enthusiasm: the Spirit is always the Holy Spirit of God who blows when and where s/he wills. And there is one thing in particular for which the Spirit is certainly not appropriate: for justifying absolute power in doctrine and rule, unfounded dogmatic laws of faith or even a pious fanaticism and false security of faith. No, no one – no bishop nor professor, no pastor nor lay person – 'possesses' the Spirit, but anyone may constantly call on the Spirit anew, 'Come, Holy Spirit'.

But because I set my hope on this Spirit, if with good reason I cannot believe *in* the church, I can believe in the Spirit of God and Jesus Christ within this church, which consists of fallible people like myself. And because I set my hope on this Spirit, I am preserved from turning my back on the church in resignation or cynicism. Because I set my hope on this Spirit, with a good conscience, despite everything, I can say: I believe the holy church: *credo sanctam ecclesiam.*

VI

Resurrection of the Dead and Eternal Life

After Galileo, can we still believe in heaven? For many people at that time that was a dangerous question. We may recall that Giordano Bruno was condemned in 1600, Copernicus in 1616 and Galileo in 1633. Even René Descartes, the founder of modern philosophy, did not dare to publish his post-Copernican *Tractate on the World or Light* (*Traité du monde ou de la lumière*), which was already prepared for printing, as the decision approved by the pope himself would be carried through with all the power of the inquisitors and the nuncios.

But the intellectual price paid by the church was a high one. And the condemnation of Galileo and thus the loss of the world of modern philosophy and science has not unjustly been set alongside the East-West schism and the division of belief at the Reformation as the third greatest catastrophe of church history in the second millennium. As Descartes wrote in a letter at the time, 'I think that to try to derive from the Bible knowledge of truths which belong only to human sciences, and which are useless for our salvation, is to apply the holy Scripture to a purpose for which God did not give it, and so to abuse it'.[53]

But the Roman church, now at the pinnacle of the Counter-Reformation and full of baroque triumphalism, was hardly bothered about this development in modern philosophy and astronomy. It opposed it with its own picture of heaven, now specifically using art as a means. For one last time Europe – or at any rate Italy, Spain, France, the Southern Netherlands, South Germany and Austria – were to be held together and preserved in the old faith by a single, all-embracing style of art: baroque. With the tympanum in the baroque churches the world of heaven, the heaven of the All Holy, was to be put on view – as a proof of the truth of the Catholic church. The painters got their favourite theme – just as if nothing had changed in heaven.

1. Heaven as an artistic illusion

In the Rome of Bernini and Borromini, half a century after the condemnation of Galileo, the famous Jesuit painter Andrea Pozzo (1642-1770) from Trent, the city of the Council, who died in Vienna, decorated the giant nave of the Roman Jesuit church of San Ignazio with a unique fresco, painted with perfect technique and a precisely calculated perspective. Today this is regarded not only as his main work but at the same time as a high point of late baroque illusionist ceiling painting: the welcoming of Ignatius, the founder of the order, into heaven, and the dissemination of the divine love through him to all four corners of the earth. The real architecture of this nave quite naturally turns into pseudo-architecture resembling a triumphal arch, populated by saints and angels. But in the midst, above clouds, heaven opens, so that one can see not only Ignatius, the founder of the order, being welcomed here, but the Trinity itself: God the Father, Christ with the cross, and the Spirit in the form of a dove. From them emanates a light-ray of love, straight at the heart of Ignatius, from where, divided into four, it goes out to all four corners of the earth with their representatives. Truly, the spirit of the Counter-Reformation and the world-wide claim of the Propaganda has never been expressed in pictorial form with greater solemnity and more powerful expressive force. This is an unprecedented apotheosis of a saint, the unsurpassed glorification of an order, a *theatrum sanctum* of the one true church and – fifty years after the condemnation of Galileo – a baroque vision of how things are in heaven: as if the Copernican shift had not taken place, as if the telescope had never been invented, and as if a highly successful epoch-making paradigm change had never come about in astronomy, physics and philosophy.

Andrea Pozzo's grandiose painting and his theoretical writing on perspective in architecture and painting, the whole of 'Jesuit baroque', had an effect especially in southern Germany, where in the eighteenth century French influence became stronger, so that here, too, from about 1730 baroque gave way to rococo (Louis XIV). A highpoint of Swabian-Bavarian rococo, still today the most popular rococo church, often called 'the most beautiful village church in the world', is the pilgrimage church in Wies bei Neugaden in Upper Bavaria. It was built in 1745-1754 by the Zimmermann brothers, both of whom were stucco artists before Dominik became an architect and Johann Baptist a painter. They were an ideal team, whose last and most significant work – after Steinhausen in Upper Swabia – was the Wieskirche: truly a sacral total work of art, in which not only architecture, sculpture and painting but now too also ornament combine equally and give way to one another. It is painted and sculpted 'architecture' at the same time. The rhythm of the soaring oval nave of the Wieskirche is crowned, as in Sant' Ignazio, by a single great fresco. But in contrast to Pozzo's painted ceiling, the pseudo-architecture here – apart for a great empty throne on the choir side and a mighty portal on the entrance side – is much reduced. Thus heaven can open over the whole breadth in a joyful blue which dominates everything, a heaven populated by relatively few people. No saint stands geometrically in the centre here, not even Mary (as in so many of the surrounding pilgrimage churches of upper Bavaria), but Christ himself coming to judgment. Theologically, too, that is the more convincing solution. But in quite a different way from Michelangelo's threatening wall fresco of the Last Judgment, here Christ appears as the transfigured Christ, bathed in light, sitting at the vertex of a rainbow which, since the flood and saving of Noah, has been the sign of reconciliation, a sign of God's covenant with the world of creation, a covenant with humankind which precedes the covenant with Abraham and even more the Mosaic covenant with the people of Israel.

Granted, here all seem already prepared for judgment: angels, apostles, Mary, the books of life. But judgment is not yet taking place. Jesus' right hand points to the cross, now overcome and bathed in glory, but his left hand points to the wounds in his side, to his heart as the symbol of love. Strikingly, none of those to be judged are present, as we know them from Michelangelo's picture of the judgment, where literally hundreds populate the picture.

Now, however, is still the time of grace, of conversion, of the forgiveness of sins. And it is the pilgrims themselves who here are addressed as those who will one day be judged, addressed by this picture of the last things which is not meant, like Michelangelo's, to instil terror, but in its bright colours in the midst of a cheerful festal space to communicate to the pilgrims on earth a deep security and at the same time the longing for an eternal home. It is similar in basic mood to a certain kind of music, the music of a work composed immediately beforehand (in 1741) by someone the same age as Dominik Zimmermann, George Frederick Handel's *Messiah*. And pilgrims leave the church with the impression of the picture at the end of the long axis directly above the exit on their minds: the mighty 'gate of eternity', towering to heaven but still shut, with an inscription from the Revelation of John, *tempus non erit amplius*, 'Time will be no more'. This too is no threatening apocalyptic message, but a joyful message to be understood quite personally, to be mindful of the time when this door will one day be open for the beholder.

'But what's the point of this illusory opening of heaven?' my contemporary interrupts. 'What's the point of an illusion of the heavenly directed towards the infinite a century after the trial of Galileo, and a good fifty years after the *Philosophiae naturalis principia mathematica* of the founder of heavenly mechanics, Isaac Newton? Nowadays don't let's be blinded by this art, which is certainly decorative in the extreme, and which in a refined way uses all the resources of *trompe l'oeuil* and every possible trick to give the impression of a heavenly world above which only apparently exists. Today we see through this grandiose baroque illusionism, which seeks to blur the differences not only between real architecture and pseudo-architecture but also between physical heaven and a metaphysical heaven. Surely such ideas of heaven are *passé*?'

Yes, there's no denying it, not only did the architect of this 'heavenly' Wieskirche, Abbot Marianus II, have to resign because of the monstrous debts incurred in building it; not only was rococo replaced by strict classicism as early as 1760/1770; but not forty years after it was finished the world of the time and its religious church system was in crisis as a result of the French Revolution. God was declared 'deposed' in Paris and elsewhere:

many priests ended up 'on the lantern'. It is almost unbelievable: at the beginning of the nineteenth century even the Wieskirche was confiscated in the course of the general secularization of the state and put up for sale; until our century it was almost forgotten. But the question of my contemporary was meant quite generally: 'What's the point of such a heaven today? Isn't belief in a "heaven" finally refuted?'

2. The heaven of faith

We cannot overlook the fact that the idea of a heaven has been radically changed by the measurements of astronomers, the sobering vistas and insights of the telescope and satellites, of space travel and space probes. Today the word 'heaven' has undergone a terminological shift which seems to make it unsuitable once and for all. People use it to express mild surprise ('Good heavens'), infuriation ('For heaven's sake') and camp appreciation ('Isn't that heavenly'). Yet even here we can still see something of the deep archetypal religious significance which the word has maintained, from the Chinese 'Ti'en' to the praise of heaven in our hymns, and which cannot so easily be replaced by anything other, better, indeed earthly. So my question isn't about some heaven over which we enthuse, into which we escape, by which we can swear. No, here my question is about a last (and first) reality in which we believe and can trust as contemporaries of the twentieth century: the heaven of Christian faith. Here I want to introduce three viewpoints which at the end repeat and make precise what I said at the beginning about creation:

1. The 'heaven' of which faith speaks is – rightly understood – by no means an 'above' beyond the world; it is not a heaven in the physical sense. Does one still have to explain today that the hemispheric vault apparently lying above the horizon, in which stars appear, can no longer be understood, as in biblical times, as the exterior of the throne-room of God? As we have heard, the heaven of faith is not the heaven of the astronauts, as the astronauts themselves attested when they recited the biblical account of creation on the first journey to the moon from the universe. No, the naive and anthropomorphic notion of a heaven above the clouds is now impossible for us. God does not dwell as

the 'supreme being' in a local or spatial sense 'above' the world, in a 'world above'; Christians believe that God is present in the world.

2. The heaven of faith isn't something out there beyond the world: it is not heaven in the metaphysical sense. It makes no difference to the view of heaven whether the world is infinite – as was long assumed in modernity – or finite in space and time, as many natural scientists presuppose on the basis of Albert Einstein's model of the world. As we heard, even an infinite universe could not limit the infinite God in all things; belief in God is compatible with both models of the world. No, the Enlightenment-deistic notion of a heaven is also impossible for us. God doesn't exist in a spiritual or metaphysical sense 'outside' the world, in an other-worldly beyond, in a 'hinterworld'. Christians believe that the world is hidden in God.

3. So the heaven of faith is not a place but a mode of being, since the infinite God cannot be located in space or limited by time. As we have heard, God's heaven is that invisible 'domain', that sphere of life of God the 'Father', for which the visible physical heaven in its magnitude, clarity, light, can only be a symbol. The heaven of faith is none other than the hidden, invisible, incomprehensible sphere of God, who is not withdrawn from the earth but rather, perfecting all things for good, grants a share in the divine glory and kingdom. To this degree Ludwig Feuerbach's interpretation in his chapter on belief in immortality was quite correct in calling God the undeveloped heaven and the real heaven the developed God. God and heaven are in fact identical: 'In the present, God is the kingdom of heaven; in the future, heaven is God.'[54]

However, any contemporary versed in philosophy will comment here: 'But Feuerbach himself, and with him the whole of modernity, are much more interested in the earth than in heaven.' As Nietzsche's Zarathustra already admonished in his prologue: 'I entreat you, my brothers, remain true to the earth and do not believe those who speak to you of superterrestrial hopes!'[55] And even if one isn't an atheist, but takes the biblical message seriously, one is confronted with the possibility of the end of this earth and this cosmos. Didn't Second Isaiah in the Bible, during the Babylonian exile, proclaim the passing away of heaven and earth:

'For the heavens will vanish like smoke, and the earth will wear out like a garment, and they who dwell in it will die like gnats' (Isa.51.6). And Third Isaiah after the Babylonian exile even promises us a new universe: 'Behold, I create a new heaven and a new earth' (Isa.65.17). What is to be said of the end of the world, since the Creed begins with creation and – according to another formulation – ends with 'the life of the world to come'?

3. The physical end of the world – brought about by human beings

A minority of cosmologists are still of the opinion that the universe has always existed and will constantly change and develop, and thus will be a universe without beginning and without end. They think that they can explain it by gravitation, electrical and magnetic forces – quite apart from the fact that there is something and not nothing, a question which this trend of cosmology attempts to avoid.

But the starting point for the majority of cosmologists is that our world is anything but stable, unchangeable, indeed eternal: as H.Fritzsch puts it, 'a world without beginning and end'.[56] At most the question whether the expansion of the universe which began with the Big Bang will go on permanently or whether one day it will come to a standstill and then turn into a contraction is controversial. Will the expansion of the cosmos go on for ever? This is the question asked again after the discovery of the oldest structures of the universe (fluctuations) in April 1992.

The first hypothesis begins from a 'pulsating' or 'swinging' universe, but has not so far been verified: one day, it is thought, the expansion will slow down; it will come to a standstill and turn into a contraction, so that in a process lasting over billions of years the universe will again contract and the galaxies and their stars will collapse increasingly rapidly until possibly – people talk of at least eighty billion years after the Big Bang – with the dissolution of atoms and atomic nuclei into their elements there will be another big bang, the Big Crunch. Then, perhaps, a new world could come into being in another explosion.

The second hypothesis, which probably the majority of astro-physicists would support, is that the expansion will go on constantly without turning into a contraction. Here, too, the stars will undergo their developments: for a while the sun will increase in brightness and then go out. As the final stages of the development of stars, depending on the size of the stellar mass, there will be the formation of weak rays or 'white dwarfs', or, after an explosive expulsion of mass, 'neutron stars' or possibly 'black holes'. And if matter from the interior of stars, transformed and expelled, should form new stars and generations of stars, in them, too, nuclear processes will take place, in which the matter within the stars finally burns away to 'ash'. Cold will slowly enter the cosmos: death, silence, absolute night.

'But don't bother us now with anxiety about something which, if it happens at all, won't happen for eighty billion years!' I must accept this interjection. The problem for the average contemporary is not so much the end of our universe, with its tremendous extent in space and time, of which in any case the biblical generations had no inkling. The problem, rather, is the end of the world *for us*: the end of our earth, or more precisely of the human race; the end of the world as the end of humankind, brought about by human beings.

Confronted with all the catastrophes, wars and famines in the world, earthquakes and other natural catastrophes, many people quote the oppressive, terrifying vision from the New Testament and worry others with it: 'You will hear of wars and rumours of wars; see that you are not alarmed; for this must take place, but the end is not yet. For nation will rise against nation, and kingdom against kingdom, and there will be famines and earthquakes in various places: all this is but the beginning of the sufferings . . . Immediately after the tribulation of those days the sun will be darkened, and the moon will not give its light, and the stars will fall from heaven, and the powers of the heavens will be shaken' (Matt.24.6-8, 29).

Indeed, today we needn't read any 'stories of the end of the world', from Poe to Dürrenmatt, to know that we are the first generation since human thought began which by unleashing the power of the atom is able to put an end to humankind. And even the relatively minor failure in Chernobyl has shown people everywhere what a large-scale nuclear war would mean: the earth would become uninhabitable. But today, since the danger of a major nuclear war has been considerably reduced by the end of the Cold War, while people still fear 'minor' nuclear wars between fanatical nationalistic peoples, above all they fear the collapse of the environment which could equally destroy our earth: over-population, catastrophic pollution, the loss of the ozone layer, polluted air, poisoned land, over-fertilized seas, undrinkable water . . . These are truly apocalyptic visions which could all become reality.

Nevertheless, here I must say to those with an apocalyptic disposition that anyone who thinks that in the New Testament accounts of the last tribulation, darkness over the earth and moon, the falling of the stars and the shaking of the powers of heaven, they have exact predictions of the end of the world or at least of our earth, would be misunderstanding the text. Certainly, such spooky visions are an urgent warning to humankind and to individuals to recognize the seriousness of the situation. But if we want to avoid over-hasty theological conclusions about the end of the world, then our starting point must be that just as the biblical protology cannot be an account of events at the beginning, so biblical eschatology cannot be a prognosis of events at the end. And just as the biblical narratives of the creative work of God were taken from the world of the time, so those of God's final work are taken from contemporary apocalyptic. Thus here too the Bible does not speak any language of scientific facts but a metaphorical picture language. Nor does it reveal any specific events of world history, but simply interprets them.

So it would certainly be a misunderstanding of the apocalyptic images and visions of the end of the world to see them as a kind of chronological 'unveiling' ('apo-kalypsis') or as information about the 'last things' at the end of world history. How many sects and fundamentalist groups think that here they have an open treasury of knowledge! And how dangerous it would be if another American president began to believe in a biblical final battle, 'Armageddon', against the 'kingdom of evil'! No, all these biblical announcements cannot in any case be a script for the last act of the human tragedy. They do not contain any special divine 'revelations' which could satisfy our curiosity about the end. Here human beings learn nothing – certainly not with infallible accuracy – in detail about what is coming to them and what precisely will happen. The 'last things', like the 'first things', are in no way accessible to direct experiences. There are no human witnesses to either the 'primal time' or the end time. And just as no clear scientific extrapolation is available to us, so too we have no precise prophetic prognosis of the definitive future of humankind, the earth, the cosmos.

So here even theologians have no privileged knowledge! However, they can interpret the pictures of the end of the world. The poetic pictures and narratives of the beginning and the end stand for what cannot be fathomed by pure reason, for what is hoped and feared. The biblical statements about the end of the world are a testimony of belief in the perfecting of God's work on his creation. The message, which calls for faith here, runs: at the end of the world, as at the beginning, there is not nothingness but God. Here the end which is announced cannot of course be identified with a cosmic catastrophe and an end to human history. According to the Bible itself the end has two sides: the ending of the old, the transitory, the imperfect, the evil – and at the same time its consummation by what is new, eternal, perfect; therefore the Bible talks of a new earth and a new heaven. This makes it clear that the biblical statements about the end of the world are not authoritative scientific statements about the end of the universe but an authoritative testimony of faith to the great destination of the universe, which has its goal in God, a goal which science can neither confirm nor refute, but which is a matter for reasonable trust. To this degree, moreover, we can also without further ado dispense with any harmonization of the biblical statements with the various scientific theories about the end of the world.

'But in this context, what about the idea of a world judgment at the end of time? According to Hegel's famous dictum, isn't world history itself the world's judgment? Or is Christian faith still essentially belief in Jesus' return to judgment?'

4. World history as the world's judgment?

In countless instances history can be interpreted like this: peoples and states, like individuals, will often after a long time and also often for a long time be 'punished' for their crimes. How many nations today still have to pay for what they did to others – for example, the Blacks in Africa or America – in the time of modern colonialism and imperialism or in the times of National Socialism and now again Communism? Nevertheless, one would be falling victim to Hegel's historical idealism were one to assume that all accounts are settled in history and that finally the divine Spirit of the world will prevail – by its judgment or its craft.

No, according to all experiences there is no complete justice in this world, either in the history of the nations or in the life of individuals. Complete justice remains a matter of well-founded hope, concrete longing. So we can understand why the age-old notion of the judgment of the dead, which was already widespread in Egypt, came to be combined in early Judaism, as already in Persian religion, with an expectation of the end: thus this was not a judgment on individuals immediately after their death but a judgment on all humankind at the end of time. Jesus and his disciples also had this early-Jewish expectation: they, too, still expected the consummation of God's kingdom in their lifetime.

But church history from the first century to the twentieth teaches us that the history of the imminent expectation is a history of ever-repeated disappointment – even, indeed particularly, in so-called 'apocalyptic' times. That is also true of ideas like those in the second letter to the Thessalonians (only attributed to Paul) of a last heightening of evil, a great apostasy before the end and the embodiment of powers hostile to God and Christ in an eschatological 'lawless one'. And that also applies to the idea of one or more 'antichrists' (individual or collective?) whom we know from the Johannine writings (the letters and the Apocalypse). None of these ideas are, as is often assumed, particular divine revelations about the end-time. They are pictures from Jewish apocalyptic which in part make use of earlier mythological motives and associate them with more recent historical experiences.

However, given all the apocalyptic enthusiasts and sects of our day it cannot be said often enough that it was the Gospels, not the Apocalypses, which became the characteristic literary form for the early church. In addition to the great Apocalypse of John, as we know, there are also a few smaller apocalypses in the New Testament, which shows that apocalyptic writings were quite widespread in the early Christian communities. But the decisive thing is that they were incorporated into the Gospels (cf. Mark 13) and thus as it were domesticated. Theologically, the result was a not inconsiderable shift in accent: from then on apocalyptic was understood in the light of the gospel and not vice versa. It represented a framework for understanding and envisaging a particular situation, which is to be distinguished from what is meant, from the message itself.

What is the issue for us Christians? The apocalypses in the Gospels are wholly focussed on the appearing of Jesus, who is now clearly identical with the apocalyptic Son of Man, expected for judgment. So their 'content' is that the judge is none other than Jesus, and precisely this is the great sign of hope for all those who rely on him. Why hope? Because the one who proclaimed the new criteria and values in the Sermon on the Mount will be the one who calls us to account at the end by the same criteria! At our end, but also at the end of humankind – rather as in Michelangelo's powerful fresco.

As far as Michelangelo's monumental 'Last Judgment' is concerned, it has to be said that even the most brilliant art remains what it is – art. In other words, even the biblical picture of the gathering of all humankind (just think even of the five billion people at present alive all gathered in Jerusalem!) is and remains a picture. What does this picture mean? It means the ultimate bringing together to God of all people, even the poorest, most despised, most hurt and the murdered – so that justice is done at last. It is thus a gathering of all humanity to its creator, judge, perfecter – whenever and however. As I explained earlier, even the encounter of the individual with God in death has the character of a critical division, review, purification, judgment and consummation.

'So if I understand rightly,' a contemporary observes here, 'we can confidently throw this image of the Last Judgment on the scrap heap. But to be consistent, doesn't that also rule out the statement in the creed about a return of Christ?'

Certainly not! The biblical notion of judgment as such, represented throughout the New Testament, cannot be abandoned. The biblical image of a Last Judgment still remains a powerfully expressive one. In a concentrated picture, here much becomes clear about the meaning and goal both of individual human life and human history as a whole which is also relevant for people today:

1. All political and religious institutions, traditions and authorities stand under God's judgment and will not escape it, no matter how history goes on. So all that exists has a provisional character.

2. Even my own obscure and ambivalent existence, like the deeply divided history of humankind, calls for a final clarification, the manifestation of a final meaning; I too cannot ultimately judge my life and history, nor can I leave a judgment on it to any other human tribunal. Judgment is God's affair.

3. However, the true consummation and true happiness of humankind can only come about if not only I and the present generation but also former generations and the next generation, the one after that and the last one, indeed all human beings, share in this happiness.

4. My life will be finally filled with meaning, and human history will come to a happy ending, only in an encounter with the manifest reality of God: the ambiguity of life and all that is negative will certainly not be overcome by world history, but only by God himself.

5. However, for Christian faith on the way to consummation,- the sure, abiding and definitive criterion for realizing the true humanity of the individual and of society is that Jesus Christ with his message, his conduct and his fate: in this sense the Crucified and Risen Christ is the last judge.

'But let's leave all these matters of principle. Answer the question directly: Do you or don't you believe in the devil, hell, purgatory?'

5. Do we believe in the devil?

Nothing would be more naive than to deny or even simply to trivialize the power of evil in world history and the life of the individual. It is there in matters great and small, and woe to anyone who is ever exposed to it in any form. The power of evil can be trivialized in two ways.

– Through privatization in the individual in accordance with the view that there is no such thing as 'evil' as a principle which transcends the individual, but only evil in human beings: there are only evil people. As if one could explain tbe cruelties of, say, National Socialism and Stalinism in that way! No, according to all our experience evil is a power which transcends individuals, and therefore the New Testament speaks of 'powers and authorities', just as modern sociology speaks of 'anonymous forces and systems' which can embody evil. In other words, evil is substantially more than the sum of the wickednesses of individuals.

– By personification into a host of rational, individual spiritual beings which allegedly take hold of people. As if, say, the monstrous evil of National Socialism or Stalinism could be explained by the demonic possession of Hitler or Stalin and their henchmen! That would be an all too convenient solution of the question of guilt: Hitler and Stalin as mere 'victims' of Satan. No, today we needn't take over the mythological notions of Satan and his legions of devils, which also found their way into the Hebrew Bible at the time of Persian supremacy (539-331 BCE). Belief in demons in Jewish faith is a late, secondary element which moreover no longer has a role in later Judaism and particularly in contemporary Judaism.

And what about Jesus? Although he lived in a time of massive belief in demons, strikingly Jesus gives no indication of any dualism of Persian provenance, in which God and the devil strive at the same level for the world and humankind. He doesn't preach the threatening message of the rule of Satan but the good news of the rule of God. In particular his healings and expulsions of demons – at that time any diseases and particularly mental disease (like epilepsy) were attributed to some demon – show his concern and where the accent of his proclamation lies: on the healing, liberating rule of God which makes people whole. Conversely, that means that the rule of demons is at an end. Luke reports a saying that Satan has fallen from heaven like lightning. So with Jesus the expulsion of demons doesn't mean the confirmation of the power of demons; it'is a bit of de-demonizing and de-mythologizing of human beings and the world, and liberation to true humanity and psychological health. God's kingdom is a good creation. Jesus seeks to liberate those possessed by psychological drives and in so doing breaks through the vicious circle of psychological disturbance, belief in the devil and social contempt.

It is above all to the credit of the Catholic theologian Herbert Haag that – of course without denying the power of evil in the world – he has clearly dismissed this kind of personified evil, belief in the devil, which has done incalulable harm.[57] And it would be foolish indeed to accept that dualistic schematism which unthinkingly presupposes that since one believes in a personal God one must also believe in a personal devil; since there is a heaven there must be a hell; and since there is eternal life there must also be eternal suffering. As if because there is something, there must also be a nothing which goes with it: because there is love there is always also hate! No, God does not need an anti-God to be God. So rightly there is no mention of the devil in the Apostles' Creed.

'But surely there are clear statements in the Bible about an eternal hell,' some contemporaries will insist. 'Or if one dismisses the idea of the devil, to be consistent mustn't one also consistently dismiss the idea of hell?'

6. An eternal hell?

Some theologians when asked directly about hell tend to give confused, evasive answers on the subject: they say that it is 'no longer on the agenda'. They hardly dare to repeat the old mythological notions, but they avoid giving a clear new answer – that is an easy way of making oneself unpopular in one's own church. That is true not only for the Catholic Church, in which up to the Second Vatican Council the allegedly infallible doctrine of the Council of Florence was put forward, according to which anyone 'outside the Catholic church ... will incur the eternal fire which is prepared for the devil and his angels'.[58] It also applies to the Lutheran Church, in which Luther's belief in the devil and anxiety about hell has played a major role right down to the twentieth century, as for example in the widely-noted dispute over hell in the Norwegian church in the 1950s.

But here I want to give a clear, though carefully stated, answer. 'Fear of hell' has now become proverbial, and had my concern been to instil the fear of hell it would have been easy for me to have chosen another picture than the hopeful picture of judgment in the Wieskirche: for example Luca Signorelli's 'Fall of the Damned' in the cathedral of Orvieto or the pictures of Hieronymus Bosch, or even – in literature – the vivid pictures from Dante's *Inferno*. But when I think how many sex and guilt complexes, anxieties about sin and penance, have been associated with these pictures, and to what extent the power of the church over souls down the centuries has been secured by the fear of eternal damnation, then with the best will in the world I cannot give any sermon on hell in the style of Chrysostom or Augustine, of Abraham a Santa Clara or the Norwegian dogmatic theologian O.Hallesby, who told his nation on the radio: 'I am certainly speaking this evening to many who know that they are not converted. You know that if you fell to the ground dead, you would go straight to hell.'[59]

This fear of hell has all too often produced intimidated, terrified Christians who were anxious and therefore also caused anxiety. What often oppressed pious dogmatic theologians and moralists themselves – repressed sexuality, aggression, doubts – they fought against in others by way of compensation. Any means seemed justified to save themselves and others – especially Jews, heretics, unbelievers, witches – from hell. They proceeded against all those they thought worthy of damnation, who were destined for hell-fire, with sword, torture, and time and again with fire. By the death of the body in this world, perhaps the soul could still be saved for the world to come. Forcible conversions, the burning of heretics, pogroms of the Jews, crusades, witch-hunts, religious wars in the name of a 'religion of love' have cost millions of human lives. Truly, before the appearance of the judge of the world the church itself has already mercilessly carried out the Last Judgment conjured up by the sequence *Dies irae, dies illa* ('Day of wrath and day of mourning'), which Pope Pius V, a former Roman Grand Inquisitor, introduced into the mass for the dead in 1570. And unfortunately the Reformers – themselves moulded and tormented by a belief in the devil and hell – in no way shrank from the violent persecution of unbelievers, Jews, heretics, witches and 'enthusiasts'. We can now perhaps recognize how important is the scriptural statement that no prince of the church or theologian will sit in judgment, but Jesus Christ himself.

No, it is not to the credit of the institutional church that nowadays no one is burned at the stake, but to the credit of the Enlightenment, which saw to it that the picture of judgment in the Wieskirche was presented clearly. And as for today: if according to orthodox Vatican teaching all birth control really is a mortal sin, then according to the same orthodox doctrine it would be the occasion for damning countless people to the 'pain of eternal punishment'.[60]

'But how, then, can you cope as a Christian today with this dismaying history?' some people will ask. 'Is there any way of getting over this history of hell?' An answer can only be given if here, too, we go back to our origins and make a critical assessment by the one in whose name all this scenario was constructed, Jesus of Nazareth. Anyone who looks at him will recognize that Jesus of Nazareth was no hell-fire preacher, however much he may have spoken of hell and shared the apocalyptic notions of his contemporaries: nowhere does Jesus show any direct interest in hell. Only at the periphery and in utterly traditional phrases does he speak of it; indeed, some of these may have been inserted afterwards. His message is without doubt *eu-angelion*, not a threatening message but a joyful one. People are to rely on this message, on God himself, in that trust which will not be led astray and which is called faith: 'Believe in the good news' (Mark 1.14). So here for Jesus faith has an utterly positive significance. Thus Christians believe 'in' the merciful God as he has been shown through Jesus Christ and become active in the Holy Spirit. But they don't believe *in hell*. Hell is rightly absent from the Creed.

But does that abolish the content that underlies the symbol of 'hell'? Here we must look for a more complex answer. Already in the early church there were significant church teachers and church fathers – Origen, Gregory of Nyssa, Didymus, Diodore of Tarsus,

Theodore of Mopsuestia and also Jerome – who assumed that the punishment of hell was imposed only for a time. But a synod held against Origen in Constantinople half a millennium after Christ (543) defined the punishment of hell as being temporally unlimited, of eternal duration.[61] Of course this definition didn't remove the problem. Just reflect: is a person to be damned for ever, to be unhappy for ever, to be tormented for ever, perhaps for a single deadly sin? Without any prospect of any redemption – not even after thousands of years?

'Lasciate ogni speranza, voi ch'entrate' ('Abandon hope, all you who enter here'). This saying, which Dante set above hell in his *Divine Comedy*,[62] can be uttered lightly only if one *a priori* doesn't count oneself among those who fall under it. But since the Enlightenment, and specifically since the time when education and criminal justice began to dispense with pure retributive punishment without a chance of proving oneself, many people have found it intolerable, for purely human motives, to believe in a life-long, indeed eternal, chastisement of body and soul. In 1990, in the USA 65% still believed in hell, in Ireland 50% and in Northern Ireland even 78%; but in Canada only 38%, in Italy 36%, in Spain 27% and in Great Britain 25%. Still lower down the scale came Norway (18%), France (16%), Belgium (15%), the Netherlands (14%) and West Germany (13%); right at the bottom were Denmark with 8% and Sweden with 7%. It is small consolation that considerably more people believe in heaven (even in Sweden four times as many).[63] Of course the majority isn't always *a priori* right in such questions. But it isn't *a priori* wrong either, especially if Catholic theology and the hierarchy appeal to the 'believing people', the *sensus fidelium*, the believing instinct of believers', in other cases where they feel that they have support.

But like many other theologians I am not just concerned with the idea of humanity but with something deeper: do I as a Christian really have to believe in such a God? A God who could look on endlessly at such a hopeless, merciless, loveless, indeed cruelly physical and psychological torture of his creatures? Perhaps look on, together with the blessed in heaven, for eternity? Do defenders of such a God think that because of an alleged infinite insult, in order to restore his 'honour', this infinite God needs such infinite punishment? But is sin, as a human action, more than a finite act? And is God really presented in the New Testament as such a hard-hearted creditor? Can there be a God of mercy from whose mercy the dead would be excluded? A God of peace who perpetuates a lack of peace and reconciliation? A God of mercy and love of enemy who could mercilessly take vengeance on his enemies for all eternity? I ask myself: what would one think of a person who satisfied his perhaps intrinsically justified thirst for vengeance so inexorably and insatiably?

But, clever theologians remark, it isn't God who damns people – by a verdict from outside. It's human beings themselves who from within their freedom condemn themselves through their sin. So the responsibility doesn't lie with God but with human beings. And human self-damnation and remoteness from God (not a place but a state) is made definitive by death.

But my question is, 'What does "definitive" mean here?' Even according to the Psalms, doesn't God also rule over the realm of the dead? So what can become definitive here against the will of an all-merciful and all-powerful God? Why should an infinitely good God perpetuate enmity instead of doing away with it, and want in fact to share rule for eternity with some counter-God? Why should this God have no more to say here and thus make a purification and cleansing of guilt-laden men and women impossible eternally?

Certainly darkness, howling, gnashing of teeth, fire, are all harsh images of the threatening possibility that people can fully lose their sense of life. But Origen, Gregory of Nyssa, Jerome and Ambrose already interpreted the fire metaphorically – as an image of God's wrath at the sinner. And not only in modern terminology but also already in Hebrew and Greek, the word 'eternity' is by no means always taken strictly ('which lasts for ever', i.e. endless, of indefinite duration). In the 'eternal punishment' (Matt.25.46) of the Last Judgment the emphasis lies on the fact that this punishment is definitive, final, decisive for ever, not that the torment must last eternally. And however the details of the scriptural texts may be interpreted, the 'eternity' of the punishment of hell may in no way be made absolute. It is a contradiction to accept God's love and mercy and at the same time the existence of a place of eternal torment. No, the punishment of hell, like everything else, remains subordinate to God, his will and his grace.

And at any rate it should be noted that today the question of hell should not be restricted in a privatized way to the question of the salvation of one's own soul. It refers people back to the reality in which their own hell is so often to be found. That in the light of the crucified and risen Christ damnation to hell is not the last word, but should give us power to work for the removal of the hells of this earth. As the Protestant theologian Jürgen Moltmann puts it: 'If Christ is truly risen from death and hell, that leads to a revolt of the conscience against the hells on earth and all those who stoke them up. For the resurrection of this condemned man is attested and already realized in rebellion against the condemnation of human beings by other human beings. The more real the hope that hell has been shattered, the more militant and political it will become in the shattering of the hells, of the white, black and green hells, the noisy hells and the quiet hells.'[64]

But it will be insisted: 'If a purification and cleansing of guilt-laden people is to be possible after their death, how can this come about? Surely in our century people will no longer want to believe in the notion of a purgatory which appears in some religions, though not in the Hebrew Bible and the New Testament writings, since along with the mediaeval cult of the poor souls and indulgences this was an essential cause of the Reformation?' This question also moves Catholic contemporaries today.

7. Purgatory and unexpiated guilt

The controversies from the time of the Reformation may also be regarded as settled in another respect: many Catholic theologians, too, have given up the idea of a place or a time of purification after death, not to mention belief in an intermediate kingdom or an intermediate phase inserted after death. There is in fact no basis for such a view in the Bible. Even the Council of Trent, which hoped to maintain the notion of purgatory, left open the question of place and nature (fire?) and warned against curiosity, superstition and the quest for profit.

On the other hand, the fact of unrequited guilt remains in the history of the world, which in any case is not the world's judgment. Hence the obvious question: is dying into God, the ultimate reality, to be one and the same for all? The same for criminals as for their victims, the same for mass murderers as for the masses of those whom they murdered, the same for those who have struggled all their life to fulfil God's will and truly to help their fellow human beings as for those who all their life have only imposed their own will, given vent to their egotism and in so doing have shut out other people? Wouldn't we have to doubt God's justice if everyone entered an eternal bliss in the same way? No, a murderer and criminal, someone who is impure and unenlightened, cannot in any way find a home in God without cleansing and purification.

So the answer of many theologians today focusses not on a time after death but on dying itself. Dying into God is not to be understood as a separation of body and soul, but as an act of the whole person in which we are graciously judged, purified, healed and so illuminated and perfected – by God himself. Here men, women and children are made fully and completely human, 'whole', through God and only through God. In other words, human purgatory is not a special place nor a special time. It is God himself in the wrath of his hidden grace: the purification is the encounter with the thrice-Holy in so far as this encounter judges and purifies us, but as a result also liberates and enlightens, heals and fulfils us. It is here that we have the grain of truth in that deeply questionable traditional idea of purgatory.

And as this is a matter of dying into dimensions where space and time give way to eternity, nothing can be discovered about the place and time or the nature and manner of this purifying, healing consummation. As far as prayer for the dead is concerned, it might be remarked briefly, this doesn't mean that some superstitious, lifelong prayer (and expensive readings of so-called 'masses for the soul') is required for particular 'poor souls' in purgatory, nor even a barely understandable praying 'with' and 'to' the dead. Rather, it is appropriate first of all to pray for and with the dying (perhaps also to anoint them), and then to remember the dead reverently and lovingly and to commend them to the grace of God in the living hope that now at last the dead are with God: 'Requiescant in pace! May they rest in peace.'

'But if you're starting from the basic notion of a dying into God like this, doesn't the old idea of a hell become utterly questionable?' My reply is, 'Certainly. The three-storey biblical picture of the world – heaven, earth and the underworld – and the mythological notions of a cosmic descent and ascent are no longer applicable today. True, even the thousand-year kingdom here on earth proclaimed in the Apocalypse is no longer understood literally in the churches – except in a few "millenarian" sects – yet the image of hell retains a meaning which we should not simply give up, a warning that we should heed.'

8. Human destiny

Hell is by no means to be understood mythologically as a place in the world above or the world below, but theologically as exclusion from communion with the living God, described in many pictures but ultimately inconceivable: an extreme, last possibility of remoteness from God which human beings cannot *a priori* rule out in their own case. Individuals can forfeit the meaning of their life, and exclude themselves from communion with God.

As we already saw, the New Testament statements about hell do not seek to convey information about a beyond to satisfy curiosity and imagination. However, they do seek to present here and now for this world the unconditional seriousness of God's claim and the urgency of human repentance. This life is the emergency! So human beings are fully responsible not only to their consciences as the voice of their practical reason but above all to the ultimate authority to which even their reason is responsible! And it would certainly be arrogant if people were to anticipate the verdict of this ultimate authority over their own lives.

Now individual passages in the Bible, in contrast to others about judgment, indicate a reconcilation of all, mercy on all. As for example Paul says in the letter to the Romans: 'God has consigned all men to disobedience, that he may have mercy upon all' (11.32). And those who think they know better here should listen to the sentence which immediately follows, which Paul takes almost entirely from the Old Testament: 'O the depth of the riches and wisdom and knowledge of God! How unsearchable are his judgments and how inscrutable his ways! For who has known the mind of the Lord, or who has been his counsellor? Or who has given a gift to him that he might be repaid? For from him and through him and to him is the *whole* creation' (Rom.11.33-36).

So at the end of all creation will all people – even the great criminals of world history like Hitler and Stalin – be saved? Here first of all it is necessary to make two distinctions:
– We cannot *a priori* begin from a determination of all human beings to blessedness, as was already advocated by Origen in the form of the *apokatastasis panton*, the restoration of all or even the reconciliation of all. A superficial universalism which regards all people as *a priori* saved doesn't do justice to the seriousness of life, the significance of moral decisions and the weight of individual responsibility. Above all, it contradicts the sovereign responsibility of God who doesn't *have* to save anyone, even the unwilling.
– Nor can we begin with the opposite solution, a positive predetermination of part of humanity to damnation, as advocated above all by Calvin with his notion of a *praedestinatio gemina*, a 'double predestination': some to blessedness, the others to damnation. This goes against God's will for universal salvation, his mercy and love, which wills to save everyone, even the unwilling. Here in particular we should note those statements of Paul's which at least hint that God will have mercy on all.

If we are honest, since these statements are nowhere balanced out in the New Testament, this question must remain open. We must take with equal seriousness both the personal responsibility which everyone has and cannot delegate and God's grace, which embraces all human beings. For praxis this means a twofold admonition, depending on the attitude and situation of the person concerned.
– Those who are in danger of lightly passing over the infinite seriousness of their personal responsibility are warned by the possibility of a twofold outcome that their salvation is not *a priori* guaranteed.
– However, those who are in danger of despairing at the infinite seriousness of their personal responsibility are encouraged by the possible salvation of everyone: even in 'hell' there are no limits to God's grace.

So in neither case can we prescribe anything for God, have any control over God. There is no knowing here, only hoping: 'My time is in your hands...' (Ps.31.16). It doesn't ultimately depend on our achievements before God – this line runs from Jesus to Paul – or, happily, on our countless mistakes. Everything depends on that boundless trust in God which we call faith. That remains the central message of the New Testament: a person is 'justified' before God not by his or her works, however pious they may be, but only by an unshakeable 'faith' which trusts in God (Rom.3.28). 'God be merciful to me, a sinner' (Luke 18.13).

I've been talking for a long time, almost too long, about the devil, hell and purgatory, though on the basis of the experience that many contemporaries are concerned or repelled by precisely these questions. Happily, the Apostles' Creed does not end with statements about death, the devil and hell, but with statements about the resurrection of the dead and eternal life. 'But how are we to imagine "eternal life" today?' That is the serious question of many doubting contemporaries who would love to believe but cannot. And they add: ' "Bliss" is associated with pictures of saints sitting on golden chairs, with the boring singing of Hallelujahs, in short with the kind of heaven that Heinrich Heine in *Deutschland. Ein Wintermärchen* ('Germany. A Winter's Tale'), preferred to leave to "the angels and the sparrows".' Hence the question:

9. Will we see only God?

All the great religions promise a final state without suffering. The Chinese believe in a world above, to which the spirit-soul (*hun*), now become a spirit (*shen*), ascends. And for Hindus the supreme goal of the final human liberation (*moksha*) and redemption from their present suffering and knowledge or union with the deity, which is described as *saccidananda*: an absolute being (*sat*) which emanates perfect bliss (*ananda*) in pure consciousness (*cit*).

The Buddhist Nirvana, which literally means 'quenching', denotes a final state without desire, hatred and blindness, in short without suffering. Only a few Buddhist schools have the conviction that this final state is to be understood in purely negative terms as the total annihilation of the individual. Most believe that there is positively a preservation of the individual.

The Buddha himself was unwilling to give any answer to such metaphysical questions. However, already 'an old Brahmanic text for ancient India attests the notion that the fire is not destroyed when quenched but merely becomes intangible as it enters the ethereal sphere. Indeed also in some passages in the ancient Buddhist canon... with explicit use of the image of the quenched flame, the view is expressed that the mode of being of the redeemed is an unfathomably ineffable state, and this state is occasionally even described as joyful.'[65] So in principle there need not necessarily be a contradiction between the view put forward by most Buddhist schools of a positive end-state ('Nirvana') and a Christian view of a positive end-state ('eternal life'). In both cases there is 'another shore', another dimension, a Transcendent, the true, ultimate Reality, which is indescribable. Some Buddhists therefore call this Sunyata, total 'void', which at the same time is total fullness.

So in Buddhism there is opposition to depicting this end-state, as happens in a highly sensual way not only in Jewish apocalyptic but also in the Qur'an, which sees the Muslim paradise as full of earthly bliss: in the 'garden of delight' under God's good pleasure (there is only peripheral talk of the vision of God) there is 'great happiness': a life full of bliss, couches adorned with precious stones, costly foods, brooks of ever-running water and nectar and precious wine, served by boys who are eternally young, the blessed along with the attractive virgins of paradise whom no one has yet touched.[66]

In Christianity since the time of the church fathers the beatific vision of God has stood at the centre of all expectations of the 'beyond'. Thus especially in Augustine's Neoplatonic model there is an utterly spiritualized bliss, in which human beings as spiritual beings seem so concentrated on God that matter, the body, community, the world, is at best mentioned on the periphery. At the end of his great work *The City of God*, on the theology of history, Augustine talks of the great sabbath, the day of the Lord, the eternal eighth day, which will bring eternal rest of the spirit and the body: *Ibi vacabimus et videbimus, videbimus et amabimus, amabimus et laudabimus. Ecce quod erit in fine sine fine. Nam quis alius noster est finis nisi pervenire ad regnum, cuius nullus est finis?*: 'There we shall be still and see; we shall see and we shall love; we shall love and we shall praise. Behold what will be, in the end, without end! For what is our end but to reach that kingdom which has no end?'[67]

Now in some later interpretations this spiritual vision of God is depicted as so far transcending the senses that not only some Muslims but even some Christians cannot make much of it. This is the case when according to the *Supplementum* to Thomas Aquinas's *Summa Theologiae*[68] even the heavenly bodies persist in eternal rest, people do not eat and drink and of course do not procreate, so that plants and animals become superfluous and this new earth has no flora, fauna or even minerals, but has much glory (the haloes of the saints), a fact on which the *Supplementum*, written by one of Thomas's pupils, dwells in a number of articles.

In contrast to such a tradition, which is more Platonic than Christian, it is worth going back to the Jewish heritage. Here already in the book of Isaiah the end-time is announced in great symbolic imagery as nature and human beings at peace: 'The wolf shall dwell with the lamb, and the leopard shall lie down with the kid, and the calf and the lion and the fatling together, and a little child shall lead them. The cow and the bear shall feed; their young shall lie down together; and the lion shall eat straw like the ox. The sucking child shall play over the hole of the asp, and the weaned child shall put his hand on the adder's den. They shall not hurt or destroy in all my holy mountain; for the earth shall be full of the knowledge of the Lord as the waters cover the sea . . .' (Isa.11.6-9).

At the end of the book of Isaiah – in Third Isaiah, after the Babylonian exile – there is also that great saying which I have already quoted. It is probably the most comprehensive indication of the full-fillment: this is in no way to be understood as flight from the world, hostility to matter, a devaluation of the body, but rather as new creation – whether in the transformation or the new creation of the old world, as a 'new earth and a new heaven', and therefore as our blessed home: 'For behold I create new heavens and a new earth; and the former things shall not be remembered or come into mind. But be glad and rejoice for ever in that which I create' (Isa.65.17f.). And then it is said that human beings will no longer die as infants but experience a youthful old age, that they will build houses, plant vines and enjoy their fruits

... And at the same time, according to Jeremiah (31.31-34) creation means 'new covenant', and according to Ezekiel (36.26f.) 'new heart, new spirit'.

So those are the images of the kingdom of God, the consummation of human history by the faithful God, the creator and new creator, which are taken up and multiplied in the New Testament: bride and wedding feast, the living water, the tree of life, the new Jerusalem; images of community, love, clarity, fullness, beauty and harmony. But here too we have to remember for a last time that pictures are – pictures. They may not be eliminated, but they may not be objectified and reified either. We have to remember what was said so clearly in connection with the resurrection of Jesus: the consummation of humankind and the world is a new life in the unimaginable dimensions of God beyond our time and space. And to this degree ultimately it is an ineffable mystery, that great mystery which is God himself: 'who alone has immortality and dwells in unapproachable light, whom no man has ever seen or can see', we are told in the New Testament (I Tim.6.16). How can we identify our images with the reality of God?

God's consummation is beyond all human experience, imagination and thought. At any rate eternal life is the opposite to that eternal boredom which characterizes hell in Jean-Paul Sartre's *Huis Clos* ('Behind Closed Doors', 1945) or the dead landscape in Max Frisch's last work *Triptychon* (1981): white, unchanging light on the stage, everything in a circle, pure stagnation, inexorable repetition. If there is also a grain in truth for Christians in the doctrine of reincarnation, as I have already said, then it is this: eternal life does not exclude but includes further unimaginable infinite developments in the sphere of the infinite. The glory of eternal life is quite new, unsuspected and unimaginable, unthinkable and ineffable: 'What no eye has seen nor ear heard, nor the heart of man conceived, that God has prepared for those who love him' (I Cor.2.9).

So I would want to rely, in reasonable trust, in enlightened faith, in well-tried hope, on the fact that the kingdom of the consummation is not a human kingdom but the kingdom of God, that is, the kingdom of ultimate salvation, of the fulfilment of justice and perfect freedom, the kingdom of unambiguous truth, of universal peace, of infinite love and overflowing joy, indeed eternal life.

'That sounds almost to good to be true,' some contemporaries think: 'I've seen too many people die, die terrible deaths, to believe that.' My answer is that anyone who can believe in an eternal life can also call for a different attitude to dying.

10. Another attitude to dying

Certainly, in all this we should have no illusions about the way we shall behave when we die. Those who speak boldly here and now can be reduced to speechlessness in anxiety about their own deaths. Let him who stands take heed lest he fall. Theologians first of all. We each have to die our own quite personal death, with our own particular burdens, fears and hopes. And indeed it is a scandal for humanity at the end of the twentieth century that every year millions of people still have to die of famine and war, social abuses and violent actions of all kinds, often cruelly slowly, often with cruel abruptness.

However, in our prosperous societies dying points to a quite different problem: the artificial prolongation of life which some contemporaries increasingly find a burden rather than a blessing. Given this possibility of prolonging our lives, which was unimaginable earlier, even if it is often of course no more than further vegetation, we have become aware of a whole new dimension of human responsibility: our responsibility for living also includes responsibility for our dying. Certainly human life is the gift of God, but according to God's will it is also a human task. Certainly human life is God's 'creation', but in accordance with the creator's commission it is also human responsibility. Certainly human beings must live to their 'appointed end', but what end is actually appointed? And certainly a 'premature return' of life is a human 'no' to the divine 'yes', but what does 'premature' mean in the face of a life which has been physically and or mentally destroyed?

No, it is not because the life of the infant whose body is not viable, the incurable sick person, or the one who has definitively lost consciousness, is a 'life not worth living', or even a 'non-human' life, that the question of euthanasia arises, but conversely: precisely because human beings are and remain in every instance human beings, they have a right to a life worthy of human beings and also to a death worthy of human beings. In some circumstances this right would be refused them by endless dependence on apparatuses or drugs, in particular if only continued vegetation, a vegetable existence, were possible.

The more it is possible to direct the process of living, the more responsibility lies in the hands of human beings, and this results in a change in the awareness, of values and norms, especially for the beginning and end of human life, which can be noted in our society. In earlier days, many moral theologians regarded active, 'artificial' birth control as a no to God's sovereignty over life and rejected it, until they were compelled to see that the beginning of human life has also been put by God in responsible human hands (not left to their whim). Now with the fantastic progress in medicine we have become increasingly aware that the end of life is also, more than hitherto, made a human responsibility (not a whim!) by the same God who does not want us to foist on him a responsibility which we ourselves can and should bear.

So here the discussion of euthanasia must be raised to another plane, especially for believers: in particular anyone who is convinced that human beings do not die meaninglessly into a nothingness but into an ultimate-primary reality; in particular those who are convinced that their deaths are not an absurd exit and destruction but an entrance and a coming home, will take their personal responsibility – whether as patients or doctors – less anxiously and less nervously. However, the state has nothing to look for here (Nazi euthanasia warns us against that once and for all); no power in the world has the right to decide whether or not a human life is 'worth living'. This question involves quite simply the respecting of a qualified decision of the conscience on the part of the terminally ill person concerned (or if he or she is incapable of making this decision, members of the family or the doctor). And that means:

– The doctor should do everything possible to help people, but not everything possible by artificial technology to delay death, with often unimaginable pain, for hours, days, indeed years.
– A therapy remains meaningful only so long as it doesn't just lead to vegetation but to rehabilitation, to the restoration of failed

physical functions which are vital to life and thus to the restoration of the whole human person.

– Persons themselves have the right to reject treatment that would prolong their lives.

– However, the task towards the dying shouldn't consist solely in medical measures but, depending on the situation, should at the same time involve the human concerns of doctors, nurses, pastors, members of the family and friends.

And that brings us to the central point: must there not once again today be something like an *ars moriendi*, an art of dying – as there was in former times, though in a different way? Indeed, should it not be possible out of belief in God, in God's eternal life, in our, my eternal life, to die a quite different human death, a death worthy of human beings, indeed worthy of Christians? The Christian element is not understood here as an addition, a higher drug, a superstructure, a mystification. Rather it is understood as a deepening, a sounding out of the human, which can also measure and withstand the shallows of the negative, the dark, the fatal.

No, when Christians are to die they mustn't follow the Stoics in suppressing emotions, denying passions, being emotionally cold and relaxed. Jesus of Nazareth didn't die like a Stoic, in impassive detachment, with as little grief as possible, but in excessive torment with a cry of godforsakeness. In view of this death, Christians too need not deny anxiety and trembling but – with the death of Jesus behind them and his cry still in their ears – be certain that this anxiety and this trembling too will be taken up by a God who is love and changed into the freedom of the children of God. The attitude of Christians to death will then be the attitude to a changed death, to a death which has been robbed of its 'sting', its power.

Indeed, since death has been robbed of its sting in the resurrection of Jesus Christ, there is no longer silence over the message of the eternal life in God who has shown his faithfulness in Jesus Christ. Since then believers may rely in trust that there is no depth of humanity, no guilt, need, anxiety about death and forsakenness which would not be embraced by a God who is always also ahead of human beings, even in death. From then on we may confidently begin on the assumption that we do not die into a darkness, a void, a nothingness, but into a new being, into the fullness, the *pleroma*, the light of a quite different day. And that here we shall not have to achieve anything new but may simply let ourselves be called, led, borne.

From this theological perspective, for those who believe and hope death will take on another status. Death will then no longer be just the brutal power of destruction, the quenching and breaking off of human possibilities. It will cease to be the human enemy which ultimately triumphs over us. No, it is not death that is our redeemer, but God is our redeemer – a redeemer even from death.

Shouldn't this result in another attitude to dying? Or more precisely, in the face of this couldn't even another dying be possible, at least if we are given time to die, and death doesn't come upon us suddenly? Shouldn't it be possible – certainly supported by all the skills and drugs of doctors and, one would hope, kept company and helped by good people, to die, if not without pain and worries, at least without anguish about death? By relying in all the slow breaking of ties to human beings and things wholly on one tie, the tie-back, *religio*: in all the parting – perhaps done deliberately, strengthened by the sacrament of the dying – in the hope of a new beginning, knowing that dying was always also part of Christian life? I have experienced the way in which such a different kind of dying is possible: I mean a dying in quiet composure and hopeful certainty, indeed perhaps – after everything has been settled – in contentment and gratitude for life in this time, despite all the evil. This is a life which is now in the threefold Hegelian sense 'sublated' into eternity. Negatively, it is destroyed by death. But positively, it is preserved by the death of death and thus finally taken up in the transcendent sense, taken up beyond life and death into the infinity of eternal life, a dimension which is not spatial and temporal, but divine. As the preface of the dead has it, *Vita mutatur non tollitur*. 'Life is changed, not taken away.' This is a dying in contentment and gratitude: and it would seem to me to be a dying worthy of human beings, worthy of Christians.

But for the last question of all I find myself faced by contemporaries who have still grown up with a classical catechism; this is the question 'What are we on earth for?'. In view of the many complaints about a loss of meaning and an absence of bearings,

particularly among the younger generation, this question indeed
has a special urgency:

11. What are we on earth for?

Calvin already asked the basic question: 'What is the chief aim of
human life?' And his succinct answer in the Geneva Catechism of
1547 ran: '*C'est de cognoistre Dieu*' – 'To know God'. During
my youth, like countless others I myself had to learn by heart the
answer to the question 'Why are we on earth?' contained in the
widely-used standard Catholic catechism (by Joseph Deharbe SJ,
from 1847): 'We are on earth to know God, to love him, to serve
him and in that way to arrive in heaven.'

There are so many contemporaries who find their life meaningless; so many are psychologically sick or have an existential
void. But even to present-day contemporaries with a religious
orientation, whether Calvinist or Catholic, two answers seem too
narrow still to be convincing. It is not as if the traditional formulae
should simply be thrown away like scrap iron, but they need to
be countermanded, taken apart and put together again from
different perspectives. Arriving in heaven? Mustn't we first see to
our responsiblities on earth? Even Christians today are convinced
that the meaning of this life is not simply 'God' or 'the divine' in
the abstract, but human beings themselves, the all-embracing
humanum. Not merely heaven as a distant happiness but also the
earth as concrete earthly happiness. Not just to know God, love
God, serve God, but also self-fulfilment, self-development, love
of neighbours and those far away. And mustn't daily work,
profession, and of course above all human relationships also be
included? What else would we need to add to that to cultivate a
'holistic', total view of life?

But conversely, specifically from a holistic view of life we would
have to ask whether meaning, happiness, a fulfilled life can be
found only in work, possessions, profit, career, prestige, sport
and the quest for pleasure? Will the ability to dominate, the desire
for enjoyment and the need to consume ever fulfil a human life
with all its tensions, rifts and conflcts? Let us have no illusions:
there is far more to being human than that, as anyone feels who
comes up against the limit to all activities. Such a person is then

confronted with the question 'What am I when I can no longer contribute anything, am no longer capable of any activity?' We must in fact adapt, so that through the pressures of technology and economics, of the mass media which increasingly dominate our everyday life, we do not lose our soul, our quite personal, responsible subjectivity. We must adapt, so that we do not become slaves of our desires, enjoyments, powers; part of the mass, perhaps even inhuman. The goal must remain being and becoming truly human, humane persons. To be truly a person, to be truly human could be an elementary, succinct description of the meaning of life which could be shared by contemporaries of the most different origins, nations, cultures and religions.

And the Christian? Is being a Christian no more than being a human being? Nowadays there can be no doubt among Christians that the Christian, too, has to be truly human and to stand up for humanity, freedom, justice, peace and the preservation of creation. One cannot be a Christian at the expense of being human. Quantitatively, there is no more in being a Christian than there is in being human; Christians are not superhuman. But being a Christian can represent an extension, a deepening, a rooting, indeed a radicalization of being human: by grounding humanity in faith in God and by directing one's living by Jesus Christ.

Seen in this perspective, being a Christian can be understood as a truly radical humanism which, in this human life which is so divided, this society which is full of so many conflicts, not only affirms, as used to be said, all that is true, good, beautiful and human, but also what is no less really untrue, ungood, unbeautiful, indeed inhuman. Even the Christian cannot do away with all these negatives (that would again be a fatal illusion leading to a forced merriment which despises humanity), but they are something that one can fight, endure, work on. In short, being a Christian realizes a humanism which can cope not only with all that is positive but also all that is negative – sin, guilt, meaninglessness, death – out of a last unshakable trust in God which doesn't rely on its own achievements but on God's grace.

Is not this, too, an illusion remote from reality? No, it was lived out earlier by that one who is to be the guide for Christians, 'the way, the truth and the life' (John 14.6), precisely through this decisive radicalization of being human. On this religious foundation it should be possible to achieve a psychological identity for oneself in the face of all imprisonment in anxiety, and also social solidarity against all resignation in face of compulsive pressure. Indeed it should be possible even to derive meaning from life in believing trust where pure reason has to capitulate, in the face of meaningless suffering, unfathomable need, unforgivable guilt. I myself once summed up the decisive thing about being a Christian in a short formula which since then has supported me through a life of toil and joy, success and grief:

By following Jesus Christ,
people in the world of today
can live, act, suffer and die
in a truly human way;
in happiness and unhappiness, life and death,
sustained by God and helpful to fellow men and women.[69]

The Apostles' Creed, too, ultimately focuses on a new meaning of life and a new praxis, on a way which lives by hope, which rests on faith and finds its fulfilment in love. Faith, hope, love – in that way one can express the meaning of life for Christians, 'but the greatest of these is love' (I Cor.13.13).

Notes

1. Cf. L.Badash, 'Der lange Streit um das Alter der Erde', in *Spektrum der Wissenschaft*, October 1989, 120-6.
2. O.Heckmann, *Sterne, Kosmos, Weltmodelle. Erlebte Astronomie*, Munich 1976, 37.
3. A.Lightman and R.Brawer, *Origins. The Lives and Worlds of Modern Cosmologists*, Cambridge, Mass. 1990.
4. Cf. U.Baumann, *Erbsünde? Ihr traditionelles Verständnis in der Krise heutiger Theologie*, Freiburg 1970.
5. K.Schmitz-Moormann (ed.), *Neue Ansätze zum Dialog zwischen Theologie und Naturwissenschaft*, Düsseldorf 1992.
6. J.Monod, *Chance and Necessity*, London and New York 1972, 110.
7. M.Eigen and R.Winkler, *Das Spiel. Naturgesetze steuern den Zufall*, Munich 1975.
8. M.Eigen, Preface to the German edition of J.Monod, *Chance and Necessity: Zufall und Notwendigkeit*, Munich 1971, ²1973, xv.
9. R.Riedl, *Die Strategie der Genesis. Naturgeschichte der realen Welt*, Munich 1976, 122.
10. I.Stewart, *Does God Play Dice?*, Harmondsworth 1990, 300.
11. H.von Ditfurth, *Wir sind nicht nur von diese Welt. Naturwissenschaft, Religion und die Zukunft des Menschen*, Hamburg 1981, 229.
12. E.Drewermann, *Tiefenpsychologie und Exegese*, Vol.I, Olten 1984, 527.
13. Ibid.
14. C.G.Jung, *Psychology and Religion* (1939), *Complete Works* XI, London ²1969, 6.
15. E.Fromm, *Psychoanalysis and Religion*, London and New York 1950, 15f.
16. Drewermann, *Tiefenpsychologie* (n.12), 527.
17. E.Brunner-Traut, 'Pharao und Jesus als Söhne Gottes' (1961), in id., *Gelebte Mythen. Beiträge zum altägyptischen Mythos*, Darmstadt 1981, third enlarged edition 1988, 31-59: 51, 53.

18. R.Guardini, *The Lord*, Chicago 1954, see 358ff.
19. E.Waldschmidt, *Die Legende von Leben des Buddha. In Auszügen aus den heiligen Texten aus dem Sanskrit, Pali und Chinesischen übersetzt und eingeführt*, Graz 1982, 33, 42.
20. M.Hengel has convincingly worked out the key christological function of this verse from the psalms in a first comprehensive account, ' "Setze dich zu meiner Rechten!", Die Inthronisation Christi zur Rechten Gottes und Ps.110.1', in M.Philonenko (ed.), *Le trône de Dieu*, Tübingen 1993 (forthcoming).
21. Ibid.
22. K.-J. Kuschel, *Born Before All Time? The Dispute over Christ's Origin*, London and New York 1992, 305.
23. Ibid., 306.
24. Ibid., 389.
25. Ibid.
26. Cf.I Cor.1.23.
27. Cf. F.Nietzsche, *Thus Spoke Zarathustra. A Book for Everyone and No One*, Part Three, 'Of the Apostates', Harmondsworth 1961, 198.
28. J.Klausner, *Jesus of Nazareth. His Life, Times and Teaching* (original Hebrew 1922), London and New York 1925, 374.
29. C.Thoma, 'Spiritualität der Pharisäer', in *Bibel und Kirche* 325, 1980, 118.
30. A.Strobel, *Die Stunde der Wahrheit. Untersuchungen zum Strafverfahren gegen Jesus*, Tübingen 1980, 116f.
31. Vatican II, 'Declaration on the Relation of the Church to the Non-Christian Religions', *Nostra Aetate*, no.4.
32. Cf. D.Bonhoeffer, *Letters and Papers from Prison*, edited by E.Bethge, The Expanded Edition, London and New York 1971, 361.
33. D.Tracy, 'Religious Values after the Holocaust: A Catholic View', in *Jews and Christians after the Holocaust*, ed. A.J.Peck, Philadelphia 1982, 87-106: 106.
34. Cf. J.Moltmann, *The Crucified God. The Cross of Christ as the Ground and Criticism of Christian Theology*, London and New York 1974, especially Chapter VI, The 'Crucified God'.
35. Cf. E.Jüngel, *God as the Mystery of the World. On the Foundation of the Theology of the Crucified One in the Dispute between Theism and Atheism* (1977), Grand Rapids and Edinburgh 1983, esp. §§13, 22.
36. Cf. H.Crouzel, 'Patripassianismus', in *Lexikon für Theologie und Kirche*, ed. J.Höfer and K.Rahner, VII, Freiburg 1963, 180f.
37. Cf. H.Blumenberg, *Matthäuspassion*, Frankfurt 1988.
38. H.S.Kushner, *When Bad Things Happen to Good People*, New York and London 1981.
39. Lev.10.3. A systematic theology of the silence of God as the hidden side of God over against the 'visible' side in the Word has been developed

from the Jewish side by A.Neher, *L'exil de la parole. Du silence biblique au silence d'Auschwitz*, Paris 1970.

40. Cf. I.J.Rosenbaum, *The Holocaust and Halakhah*, New York 1976.

41. Ibid., 111.

42. M.Horkheimer, *Die Sehnsucht nach dem ganz Anderen. Ein Interview mit Kommentar von H.Gumnior*, Hamburg 1970, 61f.

43. A.A.Cohen, 'Resurrection of the Dead', in *Contemporary Jewish Religious Thought. Original Essays on Critical Concepts, Movements and Beliefs*, ed. A.A.Cohen and P.Mendes-Flohr, New York 1987, 807-13: 807.

44. Cf. Hengel, ' "Setze dich zu meinem Rechten!" ' (n.20).

45. Cf. S.Schroer, 'Der Geist, die Weisheit und die Taube. Feministisch-kritische Exegese eines neutestamentlichen Symbols auf dem Hintergrund seiner altorientalischen und hellenistisch-frühjüdischen Traditionsgeschichte', *Freiburger Zeitschrift für Philosophie und Theologie* 33, 1986, 197-225; D.Forstner and R.Becke, *Neues Lexikon christlicher Symbole*, Innsbruck 1991, 228-34.

46. According to *Kirche intern* 9, 1990.

47. Cf. *Weltbild*, 23 March 1989.

48. Institut für Demoskopie Allensbach, *Vertrauenskrise der Kirche? Eine Repräsentativerhebung zu Kirchenbindung und -kritik*, Allensbach 1989.

49. H.Denzinger (ed.), *Enchiridion symbolorum, definitionum et declarationum de rebus fidei et morum* (1854), Freiburg [31]1960, no. 984: 'bonum atque utile'. Cf. K.L.Woodward, *Making Saints. How the Catholic Church Determines Who Becomes a Saint, Who Doesn't and Why*, New York 1990.

50. U.Baumann and K.-J.Kuschel, *Wie kann denn ein Mensch schuldig werden. Literarische und theologische Perspektiven von Schuld*, Munich 1990.

51. Ibid., 164.

52. Cf. L.Müller, *Die Dreifaltigkeitsikone des Andrej Rubljow*, Munich 1990.

53. R.Descartes, *Philosophical Letters*, translated and edited by A. Kenny, Oxford 1970, 60f. (August 1638).

54. L.Feuerbach, *The Essence of Christianity* (1841), ET by George Eliot, reissued New York 1957, 172.

55. Nietzsche, *Thus Spoke Zarathustra* (n.27),42.

56. Cf. H.Fritzsch, *Vom Urknall zum Zerfall. Die Welt zwischen Anfang und Ende*, Munich 1983.

57. Cf. H.Haag, *Abschied vom Teufel*, Einsiedeln 1969; id., *Vor dem Bösen ratlos?*, Munich 1978; H.Häring, *Die Macht des Bösen. Das Erbe Augustins*, Zurich 1979.

58. Cf. Denzinger (n.49), no. 714.

59. F.Schauer, *Was ist es um die Hölle? Dokumente aus dem norwegischen Kirchenstreit*, Stuttgart 1956, 23.
60. Cf. the document of the minority commission under Cardinal Ottaviani which Pope Paul VI followed for his encyclical *Humanae Vitae*, in H.Küng, *Infallible?*, London and New York 1972, 46.
61. Cf. Denziger (n.49), no.211.
62. Dante, *Divine Comedy, Inferno*, 3,9.
63. The numbers are taken from the large-scale investigation by the European Values Group under the direction of R.de Moor, J.Kerhofs and N.Timms, Louvain 1992.
64. J.Moltmann, *Umkehr zur Zukunft*, Munich 1970, 85.
65. L.Schmithausen, 'Nirvana', in *Historisches Wörterbuch der Philosophie* VI, Basel 1984, 855.
66. Qur'an, Surah 44.54; 55.46-78; 78.31-34.
67. Augustine, *City of God*, XXVII, 30.
68. Cf. Thomas Aquinas, *Summa Theologiae*, Supplementum, Quaestio 91, cf. Quaestio 96.
69. Cf. H.Küng, *On Being a Christian*, London and New York 1977, reissued 1991, 702.

Books by Hans Küng

Christian Existence

Justification. The Doctrine of Karl Barth and a Catholic Reflection
(1957), Burns and Oates and Nelson 1964, ²1981

Church and Ecumenism

The Council and Reunion, Sheed and Ward 1961

Structures of the Church (1962), Burns and Oates and Nelson 1964

The Church (1967), Burns and Oates and Doubleday 1968

Truthfulness. The Future of the Church (1968), Sheed and Ward
1968

Infallible? (1970), Collins and Doubleday 1972

Church and Change. The Irish Experience, Gill and Macmillan 1986

Reforming the Church Today. Keeping Hope Alive (1990), Crossroad Publishing Company and T.& T.Clark 1991

The Foundations of Theology and Christology

*The Incarnation of God. An Introduction to Hegel's Theological
Thought as a Prolegomena to a Future Christology* (1970),
T.& T.Clark 1987

Does God Exist? An Answer for Today (1978), Collins and Doubleday 1980, reissued SCM Press and Crossroad Publishing Company
1991

On Being a Christian (1974), Collins and Doubleday 1976, reissued
SCM Press and Crossroad Publishing Company 1991

Eternal Life? (²1982), Collins and Doubleday 1984, reissued SCM
Press and Crossroad Publishing Company 1991

World Religions

Christianity and the World Religions. Paths of Dialogue with Islam, Hinduism and Buddhism (1984), with J.van Ess, H.von Stietencron and H.Bechert, Doubleday and Collins 1985
Christianity and Chinese Religiion (1988, with J.Ching), Doubleday 1989

Art and Music

Art and the Question of Meaning (1980), SCM Press and Crossroad Publishing Company 1981
Mozart – Traces of Transcendence (1991), SCM Press and Eerdmans 1992

The Religious Situation of Our Time

Theology for the Third Millennium. An Ecumenical View (1987), Doubleday 1988 and Collins 1991
Global Responsibility (1991), SCM Press and Crossroad Publishing Company 1991
Judaism (1991), SCM Press and Crossroad Publishing Company 1992
Christianity/Islam (in preparation)

Books on Hans Küng

Hans Küng. His Work and His Way (1978), ed. H.Häring and K.-J.Kuschel, Collins and Doubleday 1980
Robert Nowell, *A Passion for Truth. Hans Küng and His Theology*, Collins and Crossroad Publishing Company 1981

Printed in the United Kingdom
by Lightning Source UK Ltd.
122121UK00001BA/1-12/A